Whether you are encountering the Japanese
in Japan or hosting them here,

whether you are facing a restaurant menu
or a hotel desk clerk,

whether you are visiting a museum
or stopping at a gas station,

whether you need directions or want to
strike up a casual conversation,

whether you have to deal with a medical
emergency or a mechanical breakdown,

whether you want to establish trust
and good feelings in a business meeting
or demonstrate warmth and courtesy
in personal dealings,

this one book is your—

Passport to Japanese

PASSPORT TO
JAPANESE

Charles Berlitz

JAPANESE CALLIGRAPHY BY
Mayumi Ogasawara Simms

A SIGNET BOOK

NEW AMERICAN LIBRARY

A DIVISION OF PENGUIN BOOKS USA INC.

NAL BOOKS ARE AVAILABLE AT QUANTITY DISCOUNTS WHEN USED
TO PROMOTE PRODUCTS OR SERVICES. FOR INFORMATION PLEASE
WRITE TO PREMIUM MARKETING DIVISION, NEW AMERICAN LIBRARY,
1633 BROADWAY, NEW YORK, NEW YORK 10019.

SIGNET TRADEMARK REG. U.S. PAT. OFF. AND FOREIGN COUNTRIES
REGISTERED TRADEMARK—MARCA REGISTRADA
HECHO EN DRESDEN, TN, U.S.A.

SIGNET, SIGNET CLASSIC, MENTOR, ONYX, PLUME, MERIDIAN
and NAL BOOKS are published by New American Library, a division of
Penguin Books USA Inc., 1633 Broadway, New York, New York 10019

First Printing, September, 1985

4   5   6   7   8   9   10   11   12

PRINTED IN THE UNITED STATES OF AMERICA

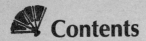

Contents

🪭 Preface

Is it possible to learn to speak Japanese from a phrase book? If one means basic communication—the ability to speak, understand, and generally get along—the answer is "yes," *if* you learn the right phrases. The secret of learning languages is to learn not only individual words, but the phrases in which they are likely to occur on a frequency basis, as the Japanese use them every day.

The purpose of this book is to provide instant communication in Japanese. The phrases are short, geared to situations of daily life, and pinpointed for easy reference, so that you can find the exact section you need at any moment.

Instead of learning about "the pen of my aunt," you learn to use the right phrase at the right time, in the very way a Japanese person would use it. And, so that Japanese people will understand your accent, all you have to do is read the phonetic line under each Japanese phrase *as if it were English.* Further practice and listening to Japanese people speaking will constantly improve your accent.

There is even a chapter on business affairs, now so important because of Japan's prominence in international trade. Use of this business vocabulary will facilitate your business dealings with Japanese contacts.

The use of this book is not limited to a trip to Japan. Besides the pleasure and help you will get by speaking Japanese on your travels in Japan, you will be able to use the idiomatic phrases you will learn from this book in Japanese restaurants and stores in other countries and with Japanese people you may meet anywhere.

Much of the pleasure of a trip to a foreign country is lost if one cannot communicate with the people one meets there. One need not be limited to English when learning Japanese can be so easy and enjoyable.

You can speak and understand current everyday Japanese with comparitively few words and phrases—perhaps 1500 to 1800—which is less than the number given in the special dictionary at the end of this book. By using the same short constructions over and over, in the various situations where they normally occur, you will acquire them without conscious effort. They will become a part of your own vocabulary and of your memory bank, and that is, after all, the only secret of learning a language.

How to Acquire an Instant Japanese Accent

Every phrase or sentence in this book is presented in English on the first line, in Japanese written in roman letters on the second line, and on the third line, in an easy-to-read phonetic system to enable you to say the Japanese phrase correctly. Just pronounce the third line as if you were reading English and you will come very close to the correct Japanese pronunciation.

Here is an example:

(English) **Do you understand?**

(Japanese) Anata-wa wakarimasu-ka?

(Phonetics) *Ah-na-ta-wa wa-ka-ree-mahss-ka?*

The suffixes attached to the words in the second line show

the function of the word in the sentence or indicate a question (see page 149).

Here are some points to remember.

1. The vowels do not change their sounds. In Japanese *a* is pronounced *ah*; *e* a sharp *eh*; *i* like *ee*; *o* as *oh*; and *u* as *oo*. Where there may be doubt about English syllables, as in *do* or *to*, we have added an *h* to the *o*, as in *doh* or *toh*. The *ai* combination in the phonetic third line rhymes with *I* or *high*.

> **Yes.**
> Hai.
> *Hai.*

2. There is no *l* sound in Japanese. The English *l* is expressed by *r*.

3. The *u* is frequently silent. In such cases we have dropped it from the third line.

> **A little.**
> Sukoshi.
> *S'ko-shee.*

4. Japanese syllables are not stressed but given equal emphasis. In lines 2 and 3 you will occasionally see a flat line over a vowel. This means that the syllable should be prolonged. *So*, both an English and Japanese word, has a prolonged sound in Japanese.

> **Is that so?**
> Sō desu-ka?
> *Sō dess-ka?*

Japanese customarily uses Chinese characters aided by two Japanese syllable alphabets. Line 2 is a roman letter adaptation of these syllable alphabets and is perfectly comprehensible to most Japanese. This enables you to point to what you are saying if you are at first not understood. But as you progress you will find it more useful to concentrate on the second line, although the third line will still be there in case you have any doubt about the pronunciation.

Have a good trip!
Yoi tabi-o dōzo!
Yoy ta-bee-o dōh-zo!

1. Greetings and Introductions

The titles Mr., Mrs., and Miss have no counterparts in Japanese. When speaking to a person, add the word *san* (honorable) to his or her last name or, if you are on first-name terms, to the first name. But *do not* add -san to your own name. Use it only when addressing another person. **San** is also used with a person's function—a waiter is addressed as **bōi-san**, a waitress as **ojō-san**, a maid as **meido-san**.

Good morning!
Ohayō!
O-ha-yō!

Good afternoon!
Konnichi-wa!
Ko-nee-chee-wa!

Good evening!
Konban-wa!
Kohn-bahn-wa!

How are you?
Ikaga desu-ka?
Ee-ka-ga dess-ka?

Fine, thank you.
Genki desu, arigatō.
Ghen-kee dess, ah-ree-ga-tōh.

How are you?
Anata-wa ikaga desu-ka?
Ah-na-ta-wa ee-ka-ga dess-ka?

It's nice weather, isn't it?
Ii o-tenki, desu-ne?
Ee'ee o-ten-kee, dess-neh?

11

Please come in.
O-hairi kudasai.
O-hai-ree koo-da-sai.

Please sit down.
O-kake kudasai.
O-ka-keh koo-da-sai.

My name is Ken Moore.
Watakushi-no namae-wa Ken Mooru desu.
Wa-tahk-shee-no na-ma-eh-wa Ken Moo-roo dess.

Your name, please?
Dōzo, anata-no namae wa?
Dōh-zo, ah-na-ta-no na-ma-eh wa?

This (person) is _____.
Kono kata-wa _____ desu.
Ko-no ka-ta-wa _____ dess.

Happy to meet you!
Hajimemashite!
Ha-jee-meh-ma-shee-teh!

So long.
De wa mata.
Deh wa ma-ta.

Good-bye.
Sayōnara.
Sa-yō-na-ra.

Jūyō! (Important!): A question is usually formed by adding **-ka** to the verb. For example, one meaning of ''sō'' is the same in Japanese and English. That's so. = **Sō desu.** Is that so? = **Sō desu-ka?**

有
難
う

2. Basic Expressions

You should learn the following phrases by heart because you will use them every time you speak Japanese. If you memorize these expressions and the numbers in the next section, you will find that you can ask prices, directions, and generally make your wishes known.

Yes.	**No.**	**Perhaps.**	**Of course.**
Hai.	Iie.	Tabun.	Mochiron.
Hai.	*Ee-yeh.*	*Ta-boon.*	*Mo-chee-rohn.*

Please.	**Thank you.**	**You are welcome.**
Dōzo.	Arigatō.	Dōitashimashite.
Dō-zo.	*Ah-ree-ga-tōh.*	*Dōh-ee-ta-shee-ma-shee-teh.*

Excuse me.	**I'm sorry.**	**It's all right.**
Sumimasen.	Gomen nasai.	Yoroshii.
Soo-mee-ma-sen.	*Go-men na-sai.*	*Yo-ro-shee'ee.*

Here.	**There.**	**This.**	**That.**
Koko-ni.	Asoko-ni.	Kore.	Sore.
Ko-ko-nee.	*Ah-so-ko-nee.*	*Ko-reh.*	*So-reh.*

Do you speak English?
Eigo-o hanashimasu-ka?
Eh-go-oh ha-na-shee-mahss-ka?

I speak a little Japanese.
Nihongo-o sukoshi hanashimasu.
Nee-hohn-go-o s'ko-shee ha-na-shee-mahss.

Do you understand?
Wakarimasu-ka?
Wa-ka-ree-mahss-ka?

I understand.
Wakarimasu.
Wa-ka-ree-mahss.

I like this.
Suki desu.
Soo-kee dess.

How much is it?
Ikura desu-ka?
Ee-koo-ra dess-ka?

It's a little expensive.
Sukoshi takai desu.
S'ko-shee ta-kai dess.

I'll come back.
Mata kimasu.
Ma-ta kee-mahss.

When?
Itsu desu-ka?
It-soo dess-ka.

How far?
Dono kurai-no kyori desu-ka?
Doh-no koo-rai-no k'yo-ree dess-ka?

How much time?
Dono kurai-no jikan desu-ka?
Doh-no koo-rai-no jee-kahn dess-ka?

Now.
Ima.
Ee-ma.

Later.
Ato.
Ah-toh.

Not now.
Ima de wa arimasen.
Ee-ma deh wa ah-ree-ma-sen.

It doesn't matter.
Kamaimasen.
Ka-mai-ma-sen.

Speak slowly, please.
Yukkuri hanashite, kudasai.
*Yook-koo-ree ha-na-shee-teh,
koo-da-sai.*

Repeat, please.
Dōzo, mō ichi do.
Dōh-zo, mō ee-chee doh.

Please write the address
Jūsho-o kaite kudasai
Joō-sho-o ka-ee-teh koo-da-sai

in Japanese.
Nihon-go-de.
Nee-hohn-go-deh.

in English.
Eigo-de.
Ey-go-deh.

Who is it?
Dare desu-ka?
Da-reh dess-ka?

Come in!
Ohairi kudasai!
O-hai-ree koo-da-sai!

Wait here, please.
Koko-de matte, kudasai.
Ko-ko-deh maht-teh, koo-da-sai.

Wait a minute, please.
Chotto matte, kudasai.
Cho-toh maht-teh, koo-da-sai.

Stop, please.
Tomatte, kudasai.
Toh-maht-teh koo-da-sai.

That's all.
Sore dake desu.
So-reh da-keh dess.

Let's go.
Ikimashō.
Ee-kee-ma-shō.

What is it (this)?
Nan desu-ka?
Nahn dess-ka?

Where is the telephone?
Denwa-wa doko desu-ka?
Den-wa-wa doh-ko dess-ka?

Where is the rest room?
Otearai-wa doko desu-ka?
Oh-teh-ah-rai-wa doh-ko dess-ka?

男 **Men's**
Otoko-no.
Oh-toh-ko-no.

女 **Women's**
Onna-no.
Oh-na-no.

Show me the way, please.
Michi-o o-shiete, kudasai.
*Mee-chee-o o-shee-yeh-teh
koo-da-sai.*

Who? **I**
Dare? watakushi
Da-reh? *wa-tahk-shee*

you	**he**	**she**	**we**
anata	kare	kanojo	watakushi-tachi
ah-na-ta	*ka-reh*	*ka-no-jo*	*wa-tahk-shee-ta-chee*

you (more than one)	**they (men)**	**they (women)**
anata-tachi	kare-tachi	kanojo-tachi
ah-na-ta-ta-chee	*ka-reh-ta-chee*	*ka-no-jo-ta-chee*

Is it possible? (or Can I, Can you, Can we, Can he, etc.)
Dekimasu-ka?
Deh-kee-mahss-ka?

It isn't possible (or I can't, You can't, We can't, He can't, etc.)
Dekimasen.
Deh-kee-ma-sen.

Jūyō! (Important!): The forms used for asking for something or giving an order in Japanese are extremely polite, typical of Japanese courtesy. **Dōzo** means "please" and **kudasai** also functions as "please." **Kudasai** implies that you are asking the person you are addressing to hand you, bring you, or accomplish something from his or her superior level.

A word you will constantly hear is **ne,** used as an affirmative question such as "isn't it?" or "don't you think so?" **Sō desu-ne?** = "Isn't it so?"

The verb form is often used by itself without the pronoun, unless the pronoun is needed for clarity. **Wakarimasu,** for example, can mean "I understand," "We understand," "He (she) understands," etc.

3. Numbers

The numbers are important not only for asking prices (and perhaps to bargain), but for phone numbers, addresses, telling time, and even for the names of the months. If you memorize the first ten numbers, you will be able to express numbers up to 100 and then, with the word for "hundred," "thousand," and "hundred thousand," you can deal with **okane** (money), **denwa bangō** (telephone numbers), and **jūsho** (addresses).

1	**2**	**3**	**4**	(or) **4**
ichi	ni	san	shi	yon
ee-chee	*nee*	*sahn*	*shee*	*yohn*

5	**6**	**7**
go	roku	shichi
go	*ro-koo*	*shee-chee*

8	**9**	**10**
hachi	ku	Jū
ha-chee	*koo*	*jōō*

11	**12**	**13**	**14**	**15**
jū-ichi	jū-ni	jū-san	jū-shi	jū-go
jōō ee-chee	*jōō-nee*	*jōō-sahn*	*jōō-shee*	*jōō-go*

16	**17**	**18**	**19**
jū-roku	jū-shichi	jū-hachi	jū-ku
joō-ro-koo	*joō-shee-chee*	*joō-ha-chee*	*joō-koo*

20	**21**	**22, etc.**	**30**
ni-jū	ni-jū-ichi	ni-jū-ni	san-jū
nee-joō	*nee-joō-ee-chee*	*nee-joō-nee*	*sahn-joō*

31	**32, etc.**	**40**	**50**
san-jū ichi	san-jū ni	shi-jū	go-jū
sahn-joō ee-chee	*sahn-joō nee*	*shee-joō*	*go-joō*

60	**70**	**80**	**90**
roku-jū	shichi-jū	hachi-jū	kyu-jū
ro-koo-joō	*shee-chee-joō*	*ha-chee-joō*	*koo-joō*

100	**200**	**300**	**400**
hyaku	ni-hyaku	san-byaku	yon-hyaku
h'ya-koo	*nee-h'ya-koo*	*shan-b'ya-koo*	*yohn-h'ya-koo*

500	**600**	**700**	**800**
go-hyaku	roppaku	nana-hyaku	ha-ppaku
go-h'ya-koo	*ro-p'ya-koo*	*na-na-h'ya-koo*	*ha-p'ya-koo*

900	**1000**	**100,000**	**1,000,000**
kyū-hyaku	sen	man	hyaku-man
k'yoō-h'ya-koo	*sen*	*mahn*	*h'ya-koo-mahn*

first	**second**	**third**
ichi-ban	ni-ban	san-ban
ee-chee-bahn	*nee-bahn*	*sahn-bahn*

ようこそ

4. Arrival

Although most airport inspectors and airline personnel will speak to you in English, you should be familiar with these useful short expressions while you are in Japan.

Here is my passport.
Watakushi-no pasupōto desu.
Wa-tahk-shee-no pahs-pō-toh dess.

My wife's passport.
Kanai-no pasupō-to.
Ka-nai-no pahs-pō-toh.

I am on a visit.
Ryokōsha desu.
R'yo-kō-sha dess.

For one week.
Isshūkan desu.
Is-shū-kahn dess.

A business trip.
Shigoto-no ryokō desu.
Shee-go-toh-no ryo-kō dess.

Where is the baggage?
Nimotsu-wa doko desu-ka?
Nee-mo-t'soo-wa doh-ko dess-ka?

Flight 301.
San rei ichi bin.
Sahn rey ee-chee bin.

These are my bags.
Kore-wa watakushi-no
   nimotsu desu.
*Ko-reh-wa wa-tahk-shee-no
   nee-mo-t'soo dess.*

Over there.
Asoko desu.
Ah-so-ko dess.

This one (or) these.
Kore.
Ko-reh.

**That one (or)
   those.**
Sore.
So-reh.

Where are the taxis?
Takushī-wa doko desu-ka?
Tahk-shēē-wadoh-ko dess-ka?

Porter!
Pōta-san!
Pō-ta-san!

Take these bags to a taxi, please.
Kono nimotsu-o takushī made, dōzo.
Ko-no nee-mo-t'soo-wo tahk-shēē ma-deh, dōh-zo.

I'll carry this one.
Kore-o watakushi-ga
   mochimasu.
*Ko-reh-oh wa-tahk-shee-ga
   mo-chee-mahss.*

Driver!
Untenshu-san!
Oon-ten-shoo-sahn!

The Hotel Ōtani, please.
Hoteru Ōtani-ni, dōzo.
*Ho-teh-roo Oh-ta-nee-nee,
   dōh-zo.*

Is this vacant?
Kūsha desu-ka?
Koō-shah dess-ka?

Where is . . . ?
. . . doko desu-ka?
. . . doh-ko dess-ka?

Say the name of the place you want *first*, attach -wa to it, and *then* ask where it is.

A good restaurant . . .
Ii restoran . . .
Ee'ee res-toh-rahn . . .

The post office . . .
Yūbin kyoku . . .
Yoō-bin k'yo-koo . . .

A drugstore . . .
Yakkyoku . . .
Yahk-k'yo-koo . . .

A department store . . .
Depāto . . .
Deh-pā-toh . . .

A movie theater . . .
Eigakan . . .
Ey-ga-kahn . . .

The address on this card . . .
Jūsho-ga kono meishi-ni . . .
Joō-sho-ga ko-no mey-shee-nee . . .

Follow this street.
Kono michi-ni sotte.
Ko-no mee-chee-nee soht-teh.

To the right.
Migi-ni.
Mee-ghee-nee.

To the left.
Hidari-ni.
Hee-da-ree-nee.

On the corner.
Kado-ni.
Ka-do-nee.

Is it far?
Tōi desu-ka?
Tōy dess-ka?

Is it near?
Chikai desu-ka?
Chee-kai dess-ka?

It's far.
Tōi desu.
Tōy dess.

Take a taxi.
Takushī-ni notte kudasai.
Ta-koo-sheē-nee noht-teh koo-da-sai.

Or, you may be met at the airport . . .

Excuse me.
Sumimasen.
Soo-mee-ma-sen.

Are you Mr. Baker?
Anata-wa Beikā-san desu-ka?
*Ah-na-ta-wa Bey-kā-sahn
   dess-ka?*

Yes. That's right.
Hai. Sō desu.
Hai. Sō dess.

My name is Toro.
Watakushi-no namae-wa Toro desu.
Wa-tahk-shee-no na-ma'eh-wa Toh-ro dess.

**(I am) from the Sanyō
  Company.**
Sanyō Kaisha kara desu.
Sahn-yō Kai-sha ka-ra dess.

Welcome!
Yōkoso!
Yō-ko-so!

How do you do?
Hajimemashite!
Ha-jee-meh-ma-shee-teh!

This is my wife.
Kore-wa kanai desu.
Ko-reh-wa ka-nai dess.

It's an honor to meet you.
Kōei desu.
Kō-eh dess.

The car is waiting.
Kuruma-ga matte imasu.
*Koo-roo-ma-ga ma-teh
   ee-mahss.*

This way, please.
Kochira-ni, dōzo.
Ko-chee-ra-nee, dōh-zo.

Thank you.
Dōmo arigatō.
Dōh-mo ah-ree-ga-tōh.

You are very kind.
Go-shin setsu.
Go-shin set-soo.

The short syllables **-wa, -o, -ni, -no, -ka** simply show the function of the word to which it is appended—whether it is the subject or object, or adds the meaning "to," "for," or "at," or makes the sentence a question.

    -wa = the subject of a sentence
    -o = the direct object
    -ni = "to" "for" "at" etc.
    -no = possessive
    -ka = a spoken question mark

Don't worry too much about these—with the repetition of the sentences given in this book, these and other suffixes and their use will eventually become natural to you—just as they are to the Japanese. To make sure you understand people's answers, you can show them the "Point to the Answer" section at the end of the book.

5. Hotel—Laundry— Dry Cleaning

旅
館

Although the staffs of the hotels in the larger cities usually speak English, you will find that the use of Japanese makes for better relations with the service personnel. Besides, it is fun, and you should practice Japanese at every opportunity. We have included laundry and dry cleaning in this section so you can make yourself understood when speaking to the chambermaid or valet and also use in smaller hotels or Japanese-style inns where they don't speak English.

Excuse me, where is a good hotel?
Sumimasen, ii hoteru-wa doko desu-ka?
Soo-mee-ma-sen, ee'ee ho-teh-roo-wa do-ko dess-ka?

A good ryōkan (Japanese-style inn) . . .
Ii ryokan . . .
Ee'ee r'yo-kahn . . .

In the center of town.
Machi-no naka-ni.
Ma-chee-no na-ka-nee.

Good morning! I made a reservation.
Ohayō! Yoyaku-o shimashita.
O-ha-yō! Yo-ya-koo-o shee-mahsh-ta.

My name is Doe.
Namae-wa Dō desu.
Na-mah' ee-wa Dōh dess.

Have you (is there) a room?
Heya-ga arimasu-ka?
Heh-ya-ga ah-ree-mahss-ka?

For one person, please.
Hitori, dōzo.
Hee-toh-ree, dōh-zo.

For two.
Futari.
Foo-ta-ree.

I wish a large bed.
Ōkii betto-o hoshii desu.
Ōh-kee bet-toh-o ho-shee' ee dess.

Two beds.
betto-o futatsu.
bet-toh-o foo-taht-soo.

Has it a bathroom?
Basurūmu-ga arimasu-ka?
Bahss-roō-moo-ga ah-ree-mahss-ka?

Air conditioned?
Reibō?
Rey-bō?

Television?
Terebi?
Teh-reh-bee?

Radio?
Rajio?
Ra-jee-yo?

How much is it?   **(per) day.**   **(per) week.**
Ikura desu-ka?   ichi nichi.   isshū kan.
Ee-koo-ra dehss-ka?   ee-chee nee-chee.   ee-shōō kahn.

I am staying three days.
Mikka taizai shimasu.
Meek-ka tai-zai shee-mahss.

Are meals included?
Shokuji tsuki desu-ka?
Sho-koo-jee t' soo-kee dess-ka?

Is breakfast included?
Asagohan tsuki desu-ka?
Ah-sa-go-hahn t' soo-kee dess-ka?

I would like to see the room.
Heya-o mitai desu.
Heh-ya-o mee-tai dess.

Where is the bathroom?
Basurūmu-wa doko desu-ka?
*Bahs-rōo-moo-wa do-ko
    dess-ka?*

the shower.
shawā.
sha-wā.

**Is there a Japanese bath
    here?**
Koko-ni o-furo-ga arimasu-ka?
*Ko-ko-nee oh-foo-ro-ga
    ah-ree-mahss-ka?*

Where?
Doko-ni?
Doh-ko-nee?

It's hot, isn't it?
Atsui desu-ne?
Aht-soo-ee dess-neh?

Yes, it's very hot!
Hai, taihen atsui desu!
Hai tai-hen aht-soo-ee dess!

I want another room.
Hokano heya-o hoshii
    desu.
*Ho-ka-no heh-ya-o ho-
    shee'ee-dess.*

higher up.
motto takai.
mo-toh ta-kai.

larger.
moto ōkii.
mo-toh ō-kee.

This one is good.
Kore-ga ii desu.
Ko-reh-ga ee'ee dess.

**Excuse me, how does this
    work?**
Sumimasen, kore-wa dō
    shimasu-ka?
*Soo-mee-ma-sen, ko-reh-wa
    dō shee-mahss-ka?*

What time is lunch?
Chūshyoku-wa nanji desu-ka?
*Choō-sh'yo-koo-wa nahn-jee
    dess-ka?*

What time is dinner served?
Yūshoku-wa nanji desu-ka?
*Yō-sho-koo-wa nahn-jee
    dess-ka?*

Hello. This is Room 565.
Moshi moshi. Kono heya-wa go-roku-go desu.
Mo-shee mo-shee. Ko-no heh-ya-wa go-ro-koo-go dess.

Please bring mineral water and ice.
Dōzo sōda to kōri-o motte kite kudasai.
Dōh-zo sō-da toh kō-ree-o mo-teh keet-teh koo-da-sai.

Please bring breakfast.
Dōzo asagohan-o motte kite kudasai.
Dōh-zo ah-sa-go-hahn-o mo-teh keet-teh koo-da-sai.

Orange juice, fried eggs, and bacon, toast and butter, coffee and milk.
Orenji jūsu, fraido egg to bēkon, tōsuto to batā, kōhi to miruku.
O-ren-jee joō-soo, fry-doh egg toh bēy-kohn, toast-o toh ba-tā, ko-hee toh mee-roo-koo.

Quickly, please.
Dōzo, hayaku.
Dōh-zo, ha-ya-koo.

Is it possible?
Dekimasu-ka?
Deh-kee-mahss-ka?

Are you the chambermaid?
Anata-wa meido-san desu-ka?
*Ah-na-ta-wa mey-doh-sahn
    dess-ka?*

Please clean the room.
Heya-o sōji shite kudasai.
*Heh-ya-o sō-jee shee-teh
    koo-da-sai.*

I need a blanket.
Mōfu-ga irimasu.
Mō-foo-ga ee-ree-mahss.

I need a pillow.
Makura-ga irimasu.
Ma-koo-ra-ga ee-ree-mahss.

towels	**soap**	**toilet paper**
taoru	sekken	toiletto pēpā
t'ow-roo	*sek-ken*	*toy-let-toh pēh-pā*

Remember to add **-o** to the thing you are asking for.

This is to be cleaned.
Kore-wa sentaku desu.
Ko-reh-wa sen-ta-koo dess.

This is to be pressed.
Kore-wa airon desu.
Ko-reh-wa ai-rohn dess.

. . . to be washed.
. . . arai desu.
. . . ah-rai dess.

Can this be fixed?
Kore-wa shūzun dekimasu-ka?
Ko-reh-wa shoō-zen deh-kee-mahss-ka?

When will it be ready?
Itsu dekimasu-ka?
It-soo deh-kee-mahss-ka?

Tonight.
Konban.
Kohn-bahn.

Tomorrow.
Ashita.
Ah-shee-ta.

Tomorrow afternoon.
Ashita-no gogo.
Ah-shee-ta-no go-go.

Tomorrow evening.
Ashita-no ban.
Ah-shee-ta-no bahn.

For sure?
Kakujitsu?
Ka-koo-jit-soo?

Are my clothes ready?
Sentaku mono-wa dekimashita-ka?
Sen-ta-koo mo-no-wa deh-kee-mahsh-ta-ka?

Good!
Ii desu.
Ee'ee dess.

My key, please.
Watakushi-no kagi-o, kudasai.
Wa-tahk-shee-no ka-ghee-o, koo-da-sai.

Is there mail?
Tegami-ga arimasu-ka?
Teh-ga-mee-ga ah-ree-
mahss-ka?

Are there any messages?
Kotozuke-ga arimasu-ka?
Ko-toh-zoo-keh-ga ah-ree-
mahss-ka?

Please send these letters for me.
Kono tegami-o okutte kudasai.
Ko-no teh-ga-mee-o o-koot-teh koo-da-sai.

How much are the stamps?
Kitte-wa ikura desu-ka?
Keet-teh-wa ee-koo-ra dess-ka?

Put the charge on my bill.
Watakushi-no kanjō-ni irete
kudasai.
Wa-tahk-shee-no kahn-jō-nee
ee-reh-teh koo-da-sai.

I have a business meeting this afternoon.
Go-go ni shigoto-no kaigi-ga arimasu.
Go-go nee shee-go-toh-no ka-ee-ghee-ga ah-ree-mahss.

I need an interpreter.
Tsūyaku-o hoshii desu.
T'soō-ya-koo-o ho-shee'ee
dess.

My bill, please.
Kanjō-o, kudasai.
Kahn-jō-o, koo-da-sai.

I am leaving tomorrow morning.
Ashita-no asa tachimasu.
Ah-shee-ta-no ah-sa ta-chee-mahss.

Please call me at seven o'clock?
Shichi-ji-ni denwa-o kudasai?
Shee-chee-jee-nee den-wa-o koo-da-sai?

It is very important.
Taihen jūyō desu.
Tai-hen joō-yō dess.

6. Time: Hours— Days—Months

時
間

On the preceding page you learned that to say "o'clock" you add **ji** after the number of the hour, and to say "at" anytime you add a **ni** after the **ji**. The following section shows you how to tell time in greater detail, including dates. You can make all sorts of arrangements with people by indicating the hour, the day, or the date, and adding the phrase "Is that all right?"—**ii desu-ka?**

What time is it?
Nan-ji desu-ka?
Nahn-jee dess-ka?

It is one o'clock.
Ichi-ji desu.
Ee-chee-jee dess.

It is six o'clock.
Roku-ji desu.
Ro-koo-jee dess.

Half-past six.
Roku-ji han.
Ro-koo-jee hahn.

Fifteen minutes after two.
Ni-ji jūgo fun sugi.
Nee-jee jōō-go foon soo-ghee.

Fifteen minutes to three.
San-ji jūgo fun mae.
Sahn-jee jōō-go foon mah-eh.

I (he, she, we, etc.) will come at exactly nine o'clock.
Chōdo kuji-ni kimasu.
Chō-doh koo-jee-nee kee-mahss.

To make sure who will come, use pronouns on page 16.

morning	**noon**	**afternoon**
asa	shō-go	gogo
ah-sa	*shō-go*	*go-go*

evening	**night**
yūgata	yoru
yoō-ga-ta	*yo-roo*

today	**tomorrow**	**tomorrow evening**
konnichi (or) kyō	ashita	ashita no bahn
kohn-nee-chee	*ah-shee-ta*	*ah-shee-ta no bahn*
(*k'yō*)		

yesterday	**last night**
sakujitsu	sakuban
sa-koo-jit-soo	*sa-koo-bahn*

this week	**last week**	**next week**
konshū	senshū	raishū
kohn-shoō	*sen-shoō*	*rai-shoō*

this month	**this year**	**last year**	**next year**
kongetsu	kotoshi	sakunen	rainen
kohn-get-soo	*ko-toh-shee*	*sa-koo-nen*	*rai-nen*

I will return next year.
Rainen kaerimasu.
Rai-nen ka-eh-ree-mahss.

What year?	**1986**
Nan nen?	Sen kyū hyaku hachi jū roku
Nahn nen?	nen
	Sen k'yoo h'ya-koo ha-chee
	joō ro-koo nen

Monday	**Tuesday**	**Wednesday**
Getsu-yōbi	Ka-yōbi	Sui-yōbi
Gets-yō-bee	*Ka-yō-bee*	*Swee-yō-bee*

Thursday	**Friday**	**Saturday**	**Sunday**
Moku-yōbi	Kin-yōbi	Do-yōbi	Nichi-yōbi
Mo-koo-yō-bee	*Kin-yō-bee*	*Doh-yō-bee*	*Nee-chee-yō -bee*

What day?	**On Monday.**	**Next Tuesday.**
Nan nichi?	Getsu yōbi-ni.	Tsugi-no Kayōbi.
Nahn nee-chee?	*Gets-yō-bee-nee.*	*T'soo-ghee-no Ka-yō-bee.*

The names of the months are easy. They are composed by the numbers 1 to 12 followed by **gatsu.**

January	**February**	**March**
Ichi gatsu	Ni gatsu	San gatsu
Ee-chee gaht-soo	*Nee gaht-soo*	*Sahn gaht-soo*

April	**May**	**June**
Shi gatsu	Go gatsu	Roku gatsu
Shee gaht-soo	*Go gaht-soo*	*Ro-koo gaht-soo*

July	**August**	**September**
Shichi gatsu	Hachi gatsu	Ku gatsu
She-chee gaht-soo	*Ha-chee gaht-soo*	*Koo gaht-soo*

October	**November**	**December**
Jū gatsu	Jū ichi gatsu	Jū ni gatsu
Joō gaht-soo	*Joō ee-chee gaht-soo*	*Joō nee gaht-soo*

Merry Christmas!
Kurisumasu Omedetō!
Koo-ree-soo-mahss O-meh-deh-tōh!

Happy New Year!
O Shō-gatsu Omedetō!
*O Shō-ga-t'soo O-meh-
deh-tōh!*

Happy Birthday!
Otan-jōbi Omedetō!
*O-tahn-jō-bee O-meh-
deh-tōh!*

Special local festivals and holidays are celebrated through-out Japan, all of them colorful and interesting to see. There are two important Buddhist holidays at the beginning of spring (**Haru-no Higan**) and autumn (**Aki-no Higan**). The Emperor's birthday is also a holiday (**Tenchō setsu**), which varies with the birthdate of the reigning Emperor.

7. Money

Where can I change money?
Okane-o doko-de kaemasu-ka?
O-ka-neh-o doh-ko-deh ka-eh-mahss-ka?

Can I change dollars?   **Yen . . .**
Doru-o kaemasu-ka?   En . . .
Doh-roo-o ka-eh-mahss-ka?   *En . . .*

Where is there a bank?
Ginkō-wa doko desu-ka?
Ghin-kō-wa doh-ko dess-ka?

What time does the bank open?
Ginkō-wa nanji-ni akimasu-ka?
Gheen-kō-wa nahn-jee-nee ah-kee-mahss-ka?

What time does the bank close?
Ginkō-wa nanji-ni shimemasu-ka?
Gheen-kō-wa nahn-jee-nee shee-meh-mahss-ka?

What is the dollar rate?
Doru-wa ikura desu-ka?
Doh-roo-wa ee-koo-ra dess-ka?

One dollar is 220 yen.
Ichi doru-wa ni-hyaku ni-jū en desu.
Ee-chee doh-roo-wa nee-h'ya-koo nee-joō en dess.

I want to change $100.00.
Hyaku doru kaetai desu.
H'ya-koo doh-roo ka-eh-tai dess.

Do you take traveler's checks?
Toraberāsu chekku-o torimasu-ka?
To-ra-beh-rā-soo chek-koo-o toh-ree-mahss-ka?

Of course.
Mochiron.
Mo-chee-rohn.

Sorry, we don't accept them here.
Sumimasen, koko-de wa uketorimasen.
Soo-mee-ma-sen, ko-ko-deh wa oo-keh-toh-ree-ma-sen.

Is a personal check acceptable?
Watakushi-no kogitte-wa yoi desu-ka?
Wa-ta-koo-she-no ko-ghee-teh-wa yo-ii dess-ka?

Have you identification?
Mibunshōmeisho-ga arimasu-ka?
Mee-boon-shō-mey-sho-ga ah-ree-mahss-ka?

Yes. This is my passport.
Hai. Kore-wa watakushi-no pasupōto desu.
Hai. Ko-reh-wa wa-ta-koo-shee-no pahs-pō-toh dess.

It's o.k.
Yoroshii desu.
Yo-ro-she'ee dess.

In five hundred-yen notes, please.
Go-hyaku en satsu-o, dōzo.
Go-h'ya-koo en sa-t'soo-o, dōh-zo.

Please give me small change.
Chiisai okane-o kudasai.
Chee-sai o-ka-neh-o koo-da-sai.

8. Basic Foods

The foods and drinks mentioned in this section will enable you to be well-fed in Japan. The section that follows this will deal with special foods you will encounter in Japanese restaurants, now increasingly popular throughout the world.

breakfast	**orange juice**	**grapefruit**
asagohan	orenji jiūsu	grēpu frūtsu
ah-sa-go-hahn	*oh-ren-jee joō-soo*	*grēy-poo froō-t'soo.*

eggs	**fried**	**scrambled**
tamago	furaido	skuramburu
ta-ma-go	*fry-doh*	*skoo-rahm-boo-roo*

omelet	**with bacon**	**toast**
omuretsu	bēkon to issho ni	tōsuto
oh-moo-reh-t'soo	*bēh-kohn toh ee-sho nee*	*tōhs-toh*

bread	**marmalade**
pan	māmareido
pahn	*mā-ma-rei-doh*

coffee	**with cream**	**with milk**	**with sugar**
kōhī	kurīmu-to	miruku-to	satō-to
kō-heē	*kreē-moo-toh*	*mee-roo-koo-toh*	*sa-tōh-toh*

tea	**chocolate**	**No, thank you.**
ocha	chokorēto	Iie, arigatō.
oh-cha	*cho-ko-rēh-toh*	*Ee-yeh, ah-ree-ga-tōh.*

lunch	**dinner**
hiru gohan	yū gohan
hee-roo go-hahn	*yoō go-hahn*

Excuse me, where is a good restaurant?
Sumimasen, ii restoran-wa doko desu-ka?
Soo-mee-ma-sen, ee'ee res-toh-rahn-wa doh-ko dess-ka?

Japanese (style) restaurant	**Chinese (style) restaurant**
Nihon ryōri-ya	Chūka ryōri-ya
Nee-hohn r'yō-ree-ya	*Choō-ka r'yō-ree-ya*

Please, is there a table (free)?
Dōzo, tēburu-ga arimasu-ka?
Dōh-zo, tēh-boo-roo-ga ah-ree-mahss-ka?

Yes, there is.	**This way, please.**
Hai, arimasu.	Kochira-ni, dōzo.
Hai, ah-ree-mahss.	*Ko-chee-ra-nee, dōh-zo.*

What's good today?
Kyō-wa nani-ga oishii desu-ka?
K'yō-wa na-nee-ga o-ee-shee'ee dess-ka?

What is this?
Kore-wa nan desu-ka?
Kò-reh-wa nahn dess-ka?

Is it soup?	**fish**	**seafood**	**meat**
Sūpu desu-ka?	sakana	kaisui rui	niku
Soō-poo dess-ka?	*sa-ka-na*	*kai-soo-ee r'wee*	*nee-koo*

chicken	**pork**	**veal**	**beef**
tori	buta	ko-ushi	gyūniku
toh-ree	*boo-ta*	*ko-oo-shee*	*g'yōō-nee-koo*

steak	**well done**	**medium**	**rare**
sutēki	yoku yaite	chūkurai	nama
soo-tēy-kee	*yo-koo yai-teh*	*choō-koo-rai*	*na-ma*

bread	**butter**	**salad**	**rice**
pan	batā	salada	gohan
pahn	*ba-tā*	*sa-la-da*	*go-hahn*

vegetables	**potatoes**	**fried potatoes**
yasai	poteto	furaido poteto
ya-sai	*po-teh-toh*	*fry-doh po-teh-toh*

beans	**peas**	**carrots**
mame	endō	ninjin
ma-mey	*en-dōh*	*nin-jin*

salt	**pepper**	**sugar**
shio	koshō	satō
shee-yo	*ko-shō*	*sa-tōh*

wine	**white**	**red**
budōshu	shiroi	akai
boo-dōh-shoo	*shee-ro-ee*	*ah-kai*

sake	**beer**	**whiskey and soda**
sake	bīru	uiskī to sōda
sa-keh	*bēē-roo*	*whees-kēē toh sō-da*

fruit	**cake**	**ice cream**	**cheese**
kudamono	kēki	aisukurīmu	chīzu
koo-da-mo-no	*kēh-kee*	*eyss krēē-moo*	*chēē-zu*

Demitasse
Demitasu kōhī
Deh-mee-ta-soo kō-hee

A little more, please.
Mō sukoshi, kudasai.
Mō s'ko-shee, koo-da-sai.

That's enough, thanks.
Jyūbun desu, arigatō.
*J'yoō-boon dess,
 ah-ree-ga-tōh.*

Waiter, please.
Bōi-san, dōzo.
Bōy-sahn, dōh-zo.

Waitress!
o-Kyūji-san!
o-k'yoō-jee-sahn!

The check, please.
Okanjō-o, kudasai.
Oh-kahn-jō-o, koo-da-sai.

Is the tip included?
Chippu-ga haitte imasu-ka?
*Chip-poo-ga ha-eet-teh
 ee-mahss-ka?*

Excuse me, the bill is wrong, I think.
Sumimasen, okanjō-wa machigatte iru, to omoimasu.
*Soo-mee-ma-sen, o-kahn-jō-wa ma-chee-ga-teh ee-roo, toh
o-mo-ee-mahss.*

Excuse me.
Sumimasen.
Soo-mee-ma-sen.

Look at this, please.
Kore-o mite, kudasai.
Ko-reh-o mee-teh, koo-da-sai.

Do you understand?
Wakarimasu-ka?
Wa-ka-ree-mahss-ka?

Yes, now I understand.
Hai, ima wakarimashita.
*Hai, ee-ma wa-ka-ree-
 mahsh-ta.*

It's fine.
Yoroshii desu.
Yo-ro-shee'ee dess.

Thank you! Come again soon!
Arigatō! Mata kite kudasai.
Ah-ree-ga-tōh. Ma-ta kee-teh koo-da-sai.

Everything was delicious.
Minna oishii deshita.
*Meen-na oh-ee-shee'ee
  desh-ta.*

We'll come back.
Mata-kimasu.
Ma-ta-kee-mahss.

料理屋

9. Food Specialities of Japan

The following foods are so much a part of Japanese dining tradition that you should recognize and know how to pronounce them as well as enjoy them. We have written the Japanese names on the first line and the English explanation on the third, although the explanation cannot suggest how tasty they are. You must find this out for yourself.

miso shiru
mee-so shee-roo
bean soup

osuimono
o-soo'ee-mo-no
consomme

sushi
soo-shee
raw seafood with rice balls

sashimi
sa-shee-mee
fresh raw fish

ebi-no tempura
eh-bee-no tem-poo-ra
shrimps fried in batter

suki yaki
skee-ya-kee
vegetables and beef (prepared at the table)

yakitori
ya-kee-toh-ree
chicken bits on skewer

tori-no mizutaki
toh-ree-no mee-zoo-ta-kee
boiled chicken and vegetables

soba	**gohan**	**ocha**	**ohashi**
so-ba	*go-hahn*	*oh-cha*	*o-ha-shee*
noodles	rice	tea	chopsticks

yaki meshi	**nori maki**
ya-kee meh-shee	*no-ree ma-kee*
fried rice	rice wrapped in seaweed

And, to express your appreciation:

I like this very much!
Kore-wa taihen sukidesu!
*Ko-reh-wa tai-hen
soo-kee-dess!*

It's delicious!
Oishii desu!
O-ee-shee'ee dess!

The cook is excellent.
Kokku-san subarashii desu.
Kohk-koo-sahn soo-ba-ra-shee'ee dess.

Many thanks for a wonderful dinner.
Taihen oishii yūhan arigatō gozaimasu.
Tai-hen o'ee-shee'ee yoō-hahn ah-ree-ga-tōh go-zai-mahss.

You are welcome.
Dō itashimashite.
Dōh ee-ta-shee-ma-shee-teh.

I'm glad you enjoyed it.
Oki-ni meshite ureshii desu.
*Oh-kee-nee meh-shee-teh oo-
reh-shee'ee dess.*

Omoshiroi (Interesting): A number of Japanese nouns and verbs are preceded by the syllable **o** or **go**, meaning "honorable" or "exalted." This is why certain words including tea, chopsticks, bill, cooked rice, money, temple, bank, and others are preceded by an honorific syllable.

10. Transportation

Getting around by public transportation is enjoyable not only for the new and interesting things you see, but also because of the opportunities you have for practicing Japanese. To make your travels easier, use short phrases when speaking to drivers or asking directions. And don't forget *Dōzo* and *Arigatō!*

Bus

Where is the bus stop?
Basu-no teiryūjo-wa doko desu-ka?
Ba-soo-no tey-r'yoō-jo-wa doh-ko dess-ka?

Does this go to the Ginza?
Kore-wa Ginza-ni ikimasu-ka?
Ko-reh-wa Ghin-za-nee ee-kee-mahss-ka?

No, it doesn't go (there).
Iie, ikimasen.
Ee-yeh, ee-kee-ma-sen.

Get on number one.
Ichi ban-ni notte kudasai.
Ee-chee bahn-nee noht-teh koo-da-sai.

How much is the fare?
Ryōkin-wa ikura desu-ka?
R'yō-kin-wa ee-koo-ra dess-ka?

Where do you want to go?
Doko-ni iki-tai desu-ka?
Doh-ko-nee ee-kee-tai dess-ka?

To the Marunouchi.
Marunouchi-ni.
Ma-roo-no-oo-chee-nee.

Is it far?
Tōi desu-ka?
Tōy dess-ka?

No, it's near.
Iie, chikai desu.
Ee-yeh, chee-kai dess.

Where should I get off . . .
Doko de oriru-ka . . .
Doh-ko deh o-ree-roo-ka . . .

please tell me.
oshiete kudasai.
o-shee-yeh-teh koo-da-sai.

Get off here, please.
Koko de orite, kudasai.
Ko-ko deh o-ree-teh, koo-da-sai.

Taxi

Taxi!
Takushīī!
Tahk-sheē!

Are you free?
Kūsha desu-ka?
Koō-sha dess-ka?

Yes, where to?
Hai, doko-ni?
Hai, doh-ko-nee?

To this address.
Kono jūsho-ni.
Ko-no joō-sho-nee.

Do you know where it is?
Doko-ka shitte imasu-ka?
Doh-ko-ka sheet-teh ee-mahss-ka?

Don't worry.
Kamaimasen.
Ka-mai-ma-sen.

I have a map.
Chizu-ga arimasu.
Chee-zoo-ga ah-ree-mahss.

I'm in a hurry!
Isoi-de imasu!
Ee-so-ee-deh ee-mahss!

Quickly, please!
Hayaku, dōzo!
Ha-ya-koo, dōh-zo!

Slowly, please!
Yukkuri, dōzo!
Yook-koo-ree, dōh-zo!

Now.	**Right.**	**Left.**	**Straight ahead.**
Ima.	Migi.	Hidari.	Massugu.
Ee-ma.	*Mee-ghee.*	*Hee-da-ree.*	*Ma-su-goo.*

Stop here.
Koko-de tomatte kudasai.
*Ko-ko-deh toh-ma-teh
   koo-da-sai.*

At the corner.
Kado-de.
Ka-doh-deh.

Please wait a moment.
Chotto matte kudasai.
Cho-toh ma-teh koo-da-sai.

Sorry, we can't park.
Sumimasen, chūsha
   dekimasen.
*Soo-mee-ma-sen, choō-sha
   deh-kee-ma-sen.*

I'll come back right away.
Sugu kaerimasu.
Soo-goo ka-eh-ree-mahss.

O.K. I'll wait.
Yoroshii. Machimasu.
*Yo-ro-shee'ee.
   Ma-chee-mahss.*

Over there.
Asoko-de.
Ah-so-ko-deh.

How much is it by the hour?
Ichi-ji kan ikura desu-ka?
*Ee-chee-jee kahn ee-koo-ra
dess-ka?*

. . . by the kilometer?
. . . ichi kirometa?
. . . ee-chee kee-ro-mēh-ta?

Please come to the hotel tomorrow.
Hoteru-ni ashita kite kudasai.
Ho-teh-roo-nee ah-shee-ta kee-teh koo-da-sai.

In the morning.
Asa-ni.
Ah-sa-nee.

In the afternoon.
Gogo-ni.
Go-go-nee.

Subway and Railroad Trains

Jūyō! (Important!): The subway lines are indicated by trains of different colors.

In case you need detailed information, ask a policeman or guard:

Do you speak English?
Eigo-o hanashimasu-ka?
Eh-ee-go-o hana-shee-mahss-ka?

Excuse me, where is the subway?
Sumimasen, chikatetsu-wa doko desu-ka?
Soo-mee-ma-sen, chee-ka-tet-soo-wa doh-ko dess-ka?

To Shibuya station, please.
Shibuya eki made, dōzo.
Shee-boo-ya eh-kee ma-deh, dōh-zo.

Get on the orange train.
Orenji iro-no densha-ni notte kudasai.
O-ren-jee ee-ro-no den-sha-nee noht-teh koo-da-sai.

And if you push or step on someone:

I'm sorry!
Gomen nasai!
Go-men na-sai!

Where is the railroad station?
Eki-wa doko desu-ka?
Eh-kee-wa doh-ko dess-ka?

Where do I buy a ticket?
Doko-de kippu-o kaimasu-ka?
Doh-ko-deh kip-poo-o kai-mahss-ka?

The ticket machine is over there.
Kippu-no kikai-wa asoko desu.
Keep-poo-no kee-kai-wa ah-so-ko dess.

To Ōsaka.	First class	Second class
Ōsaka made.	Ittō	Nittō
Ō-sa-ka ma-deh.	*Eet-tōh*	*Neet-tōh*

Round trip	One way
Ōfuku	Katamichi
Ō-foo-koo	*Ka-ta-mee-chee*

Where is the train for Osaka?
Ōsaka iki-no kisha-wa doko desu-ka?
Ō-sa-ka ee-kee-no kee-sha-wa doh-ko dess-ka?

What platform?
Nanban sen desu-ka?
Nahn-bahn sen dess-ka?

Platform seven.
Shichi ban sen.
Shee-chee bahn sen.

Over there.
Asoko-ni
Ah-so-ko-nee.

Up the stairs.
Kaidan-no ue.
Kai-dahn-no oo-eh.

Down the stairs.
Kaidan-no shita.
*Kai-dahn-no
shee-ta.*

At what time does it leave?
Nan-ji-ni demasu-ka?
Nahn-jee-nee deh-mahss-ka?

Permission to sit, etc.:

Is this all right?
Ii desu-ka?
Ee'ee dess-ka?

Of course, go ahead.
Mochiron, dōzo.
Mo-chee-rohn, dōh-zo.

At what time do we get to Kyoto?
Kyōto-ni nan-ji-ni tsukimasu-ka?
K'yō-toh-nee nahn-jee-nee t'soo-kee-mahss-ka?

Does this train stop at Nara?
Kono kisha-wa Nara-ni tomarimasu-ka?
Ko-no kee-sha-wa Na-ra-nee toh-ma-ree-mahss-ka?

How long are we stopping here?
Koko-ni dono kurai tomarimasu-ka?
Ko-ko-nee doh-no koo-rai toh-ma-ree-mahss-ka?

Where is the dining car?
Shokudōsha-wa doko desu-ka?
Sho-koo-dōh-sha-wa doh-ko dess-ka?

Ticket, please.
Kippu-o, dōzo.
Keep-poo-o, dōh-zo.

I'm sorry, I can't find it.
Gomen, mitsukarimasen.
*Go-men, meet-soo-ka-ree-
     ma-sen.*

Wait!
Chotto matte!
Cho-toh maht-teh!

Here it is!
Koko desu!
Ko-ko dess!

Conductor, excuse me . . . I got on the wrong train.
Shashō-san, sumimasen . . . Chigau kisha-ni norimashita.
*Sha-sō-sahn, soo-mee-ma-sen . . . Chee-g'ow kee-sha-nee
  no-ree-mahsh-ta.*

I wanted to go to Nikko.
Nikkō-ni ikatai deshita.
Nik-kō-nee ee-kee-tai desh-ta.

Is that so?
Sō desu-ka?
Sō dess-ka?

Well, then . . .
Sore de wa . . .
So-reh deh wa. . .

Please change at . . .
. . . de norikaete kudasai.
*. . . deh no-ree-ka-eht-teh
     koo-da-sai.*

Ship

Driver, to the dock, please.
Untenshu-san, hatoba made, dōzo.
Oon-ten-shoo-sahn, ha-toh-ba ma-deh, dōh-zo.

When does the ship sail?
Nan-ji ni fune-ga shukkō desu-ka?
Nahn-jee nee foo-neh-ga shook-kō dess-ka?

What is that island called?
Sono shima-wa nan to iimasu-ka?
So-no shee-ma-wa nahn toh ee'ee-mahss-ka?

The Inland Sea is magnificent, isn't it?
Seto nai kai-wa subarashii, desu-ne?
Seh-toh nai kai-wa soo-ba-ra-shee'ee dess-neh?

Car Rental

Can I rent a car here?
Koko-de kuruma-o kariru koto-ga dekimasu-ka?
*Ko-ko-deh koo-roo-ma-o ka-ree-roo ko-toh-ga
deh-kee-mahss-ka?*

motorcycle
mōtāsaikuru
mō-tā-sai-koo-roo

small car
chīsai kuruma
chēē-sai koo-roo-ma

I want to rent this one.
Kore-o karitai desu.
Ko-reh-o ka-ree-tai dess.

How much per day?
Ichi nichi ikura desu-ka?
Ee-chee nee-chee ee-koo-ra dess-ka?

per week?
isshūkan?
ees-shū-kan?

per kilometer?
ichi kiromētā?
ee-chee kee-ro-mēh-tā?

Is the gas included?
Gasorin-ga fukumarete imasu-ka?
Ga-so-reen-ga foo-koo-ma-reh-teh ee-mahss-ka?

Where is a gas station?
Gasorin stando-wa doko desu-ka?
Ga-so-reen stan-doh-wa doh-ko dess-ka?

How much is it per liter?
Ichi rittā ikura desu-ka?
Ee-chee reet-tā ee-koo-ra dess-ka?

Full tank, please.
Man tan, dōzo.
Mahn tahn, dōh-zo.

This is my credit card.
Kore-wa watakushi-no
  kurejitto kādo desu.
*Ko-reh-wa wa-tahk-shi-no
  koo-reh-jit-toh kā-doh dess.*

Please check the tires.
Dōzo taiya-o shirabete kudasai.
Dōh-zo tai-yo-o shee-ra-beh-teh koo-da-sai.

the water
mizu
mee-zoo

the battery
batterīi
ba-teh-ree'ee

the oil
abura
ah-boo-ra

the brakes
brēiki
brēi-kee

the carburetor
kaburētā
ka-boo-rēh-tā

Would you give me a map?
Chizu-o kudasai?
Chee-zoo-o koo-da-sai?

In English
Eigo-de
Ey-go-deh

From Nara to Tōkyō.
Nara kara Tōkyō made.
Na-ra ka-ra Tōh-k'yō ma-deh.

Does this road go to Nikko?
Kono michi-wa Nikkō-ni ikimasu-ka?
Ko-no mee-chee-wa Neek-kō-nee ee-kee-mahss-ka?

Is the road good?
Michi-wa ii desu-ka?
Mee-chee-wa ee'ee dess-ka?

What is the next town?
Tsugi-no machi-wa nan desu-ka?
Ts'oo-ghee-no ma-chee-wa nahn dess-ka?

About how far is it?
Dono kurai arimasu-ka?
Doh-no koo-rai ah-ree-mahss-ka?

Is there a good restaurant there?
Asoko-ni ii restoran-ga arimasu-ka?
Ah-so-ko-nee ee'ee res-toh-rahn-ga ah-ree-mahss-ka?

I'm sorry, I don't know.
Sumimasen, shirimasen.
Soo-mee-ma-sen, shee-ree-ma-sen.

Yes, there is.   **It's name is Yamato.**
Hai, arimasu.   Sore-no namae-wa Yamato desu.
Hai, ah-ree-mahss.   *So reh na-ma'eh-wa Ya-ma-toh dess.*

Follow this road.
Kono michi-o itte kudasai.
Ko-no mee-chee-o eet-teh koo-da-sai.

Across the bridge, take a right.
Hashi-no mukō, migi-ni.
Ha-shee-no moo-kō, mee-ghee-nee.

Then, straight ahead.
Sore kara, massugu.
So-reh ka-ra, ma-soo-goo.

At the signal light turn left.
Shingō-de hidari-ni magatte kudasai.
Shin-gō-deh hee-da-ree-nee ma-gaht-teh koo-da-sai.

Emergencies and Repairs

Stop! (Your) license!
Tomarinasai! Menkyoshō!
Toh-ma-ree-na-sai!
  Men-k'yo-shō!

Yes, officer.
Hai, omawari-san.
Hai, o-ma-wa-ree-san.

The registration also!
Shaken mo!
Sha-ken mo!

I'm sorry.
Go-men na-sai.
Go-men na-sai.

It wasn't my fault.
Watakushi-no sei de wa arimasen.
Wa-tahk-shee-no sey deh-wa ah-ree-ma-sen.

Is that so?
Sō desu-ka?
Sō dess-ka?

Please come with me.
Issho-ni kite kudasai.
Ees-sho-nee kee-teh koo-da-sai.

The verb for "please"—**kudasai** is more polite than **nasai,** another verbal ending for "please," used in more direct speech. In general, politeness, even on the highways, is more noticeable in Japan than in most other countries. Probably the most serious insult current among drivers in traffic is **baka**— "fool." Nevertheless, the diplomatic use of Japanese, plus a smile, will make car travel safe and enjoyable. Here are some useful expressions for asking for help while motoring.

I am in trouble.
Komarimashita.
Ko-ma-ree-mahsh-ta.

My car has broken down.
Kuruma koshō desu.
Koo-roo-ma ko-shō dess.

Could you help me?
Dōzo, tasukete kudasai?
Dōh-zo, ta-soo-keh-teh koo-da-sai?

I have a flat tire.
Taiya ga panku shimashita.
Tai-ya ga pahn-koo shee-mahsh-ta.

Have you a jack?
Jakkī-ga arimasu-ka?
Ja-kēē-ga ah-ree-mahss-ka?

Please push.
Oshite kudasai.
O-shee-teh koo-da-sai.

That's fine!
Daijōbu desu!
Dai-jō-boo dess!

You are very kind!
Goshin setsu-ni!
Go-shin set-soo-nee!

Is there a garage here?
Shako-ga koko-ni arimasu-ka?
Sha-ko-ga ko-ko-nee ah-ree-mahss-ka?

Is there a mechanic?
Shūrikō imasu-ka?
Shoō-ree-kō ee-mahss-ka?

What happened?
Dō shimashita-ka?
Dōh shee-mahsh-ta-ka?

The car is going badly.
Kuruma-no chōshi-ga warui desu.
Koo-roo-ma-no chō-shee-ga wa-roo'ee dess.

There's a funny noise in the motor.
Engin-ni okashii oto ga shimasu.
*En-jeen-ni o-ka-shee'ee o-toh ga
   shee-mahss.*

It doesn't start.
Stāto shimasen.
Stā-toh shee-ma-sen.

Can you fix it?
Naosu kotoga dekimasu-ka?
*Na-o-soo ko-toh-ga
   deh-kee-mahss-ka?*

About how much will it cost?
Ikura-gurai desu-ka?
Ee-koo-ra-goo-rai dess-ka?

About 2000 yen.
Ni sen en gurai.
Nee sen en goo-rai.

When is it going to be ready?
Itsu dekimasu-ka?
Eet-soo deh-kee-mahss-ka?

Today it isn't possible.
Kyō-wa dekimasen.
K'yō-wa deh-kee-ma-sen.

Perhaps tomorrow.
Tabun ashita.
Ta-boon ah-shee-ta.

The day after tomorrow.
Asatte.
Ah-saht-teh.

We can fix it temporarily.
Karino shūriga dekimasu.
Ka-ree-no shōō-ree-ga deh-kee-mahss.

International Road Signs

The following international road signs are followed by the English meaning, the equivalent in written Japanese, and finally in Romaji, the Japanese adaptation of Roman letters.

Danger

Abunai

Caution

Chūi

Sharp Turn

Kyū kābu

Crossroads

Jūjiro

Right Curve

右曲り

Migi magari

Left Curve

左曲り

Hidari magari

One Way

一方通行

Ippō tsūkō

Do Not Enter

立入禁止

Tachiiri kinshi

No Parking

駐車禁止

Chūsha kinshi

Parking

駐車場

Chūsha jō

Bumps

凸凹 でこぼこ道

Dekoboko

Main Road Ahead

主要道路この先

Shuyō-dōro kono-saki

In addition, you will see or hear the following instructions:

Detour

廻り道

Mawari michi

Maximum Speed 100 Kilometers

最高速度 100 Km

Saikō sokudo hyaku kiro

Slow Down

速度下せ

Sokudo otose

Tunnel

トンネル

Tonneru

Entrance

入口

Iriguchi

Exit

出口

Deguchi

写真術

11. Sightseeing and Photography

We have combined these two important topics because you will want to take pictures of what you are seeing. If you are taking pictures indoors, be sure to ask the custodian **Yoroshii desu-ka?**—''Is it permitted?''

I need a guide.
Gaido-o irimasu.
Gai-doh-o ee-ree-mahss.

Are you a guide?
Gaido-san desu-ka?
Gai-doh-sahn dess-ka?

Do you speak English?
Eigo-de hanashimasu-ka?
Ey-go-deh ha-na-shee-mahss-ka?

It doesn't matter.
Kamaimasen.
Ka-mai-ma-sen.

I speak a little Japanese.
Nihon-go-o sukoshi hanashimasu.
Nee-hohn-go-o sko-shee ha-na-shee-mahss.

Do you have a car?
Kuruma-ga arimasu-ka?
Koo-roo-ma-ga ah-ree-mahss-ka?

How much per hour?
Ichi ji kan ikura desu-ka?
Ee-chee jee kahn ee-koo-ra dess-ka?

Five hours.
Go jikan.
Go jee-kahn.

One day.
Ichi nichi.
Ee-chee nee-chee.

Oboenasai! (Remember!): Remember, the place you want to go to comes first and the fact that you wish to go there comes at the end of the sentence.

To the old castle . . .
Furui oshiro-ni . . .
Foo-roo-ee o-shee-ro-nee . . .

_____ **we want to go.**
_____ iki-tai desu.
_____ *ee-kee-tai dess.*

To the temple . . .
Otera-ni . . .
Oh-teh-ra-nee . . .

To the museum . . .
Hakubutsukan-ni . . .
Ha-koo-boo-t'soo-kahn-nee . . .

To the Kabuki Theater . . .
Kabuki-ni . . .
Ka-boo-kee-nee . . .

To the Imperial Palace . . .
Kyūjō-ni . . .
K'yoō-jō-nee . . .

To the park . . .
Kōen-ni . . .
Kō-en-nee . . .

To the zoo . . .
Dōbutsuen-ni . . .
Dōh-boot-soo-en-nee . . .

To the Bhuddist temple . . .
Bukkyō-no otera-ni . . .
Book-k'yō-no o-teh-ra-nee . . .

To Disneyland . . .
Dizunī rando-ni . . .
Dees-nee'eē rahn-doh-nee . . .

To the shopping streets . . .
Shōten gai-ni . . .
Shō-ten gai-nee . . .

To the Ginza . . .
Ginza-ni . . .
Geen-za-nee . . .

Interesting!
Omoshiroi!
O-mo-shee-roy!

Beautiful!
Utsukushii!
Oot-soo-koo-shee'ee!

Where is a good nightclub?
Ii naito kurabu-wa doko desu-ka?
Ee'ee na-ee-toh koo-ra-boo doh-ko dess-ka?

Let's go!
Ikimashō!
Ee-kee-ma-shō!

You are a good guide.
Anata-wa taihen ii gaido-san
    desu.
*Ah-na-ta-wa tai-hen ee'ee
    gai-doh-sahn dess.*

Come again tomorrow.
Ashita mata kite kudasai.
Ah-shee-ta ma-ta kee-teh koo-da-sai.

At ten o'clock.
Jūji-ni.
Joō-jee-nee.

At two in the afternoon.
Gogo niji-ni.
Go-go nee-jee-nee.

Thank you for everything.
Iro iro, dōmo arigatō.
Ee-ro ee-ro, dōh-mo ah-ree-ga-tōh.

And, if you are seeing the sights on your own, you will find these questions and possible answers useful. And remember you can make any verb, noun, or adjective into a question by adding **-ka** to the verb or **desu-ka** to the noun or adjective.

May I enter?
Hairemasu-ka?
Ha-ee-ree-mahss-ka?

It's open.
Aitemasu.
Ah-ee-teh-mahss.

It's closed.
Shimarimashita.
Shee-ma-ree-mahsh-ta.

What time does it open?
Nan ji-ni akimasu-ka?
Nahn-jee-nee ah-kee-mahss-ka?

It opens at half past two.
Niji han-ni akimasu.
Nee-jee hahn-nee ah-kee-mahss.

What is the admission?
Nyūjō ryō-wa ikura desu-ka?
N'yoō-jō r'yō-wa ee-koo-ra dess-ka?

Five hundred yen.
Go-hyaku en.
Go-h'ya-koo en.

For children?
Kodomo-wa?
Ko-doh-mo-wa?

No charge.
Muryō.
Moor-yō.

Ticket, please.
Kippu-o, dōzo.
Keep-poo-o, dōh-zo.

This way, please.
Kochira-ni, dōzo.
Ko-chee-ra-nee, dōh-zo.

No smoking.
Kin en.
Keen en.

This is very old, isn't it?
Kore-wa taihen furui desu-ka?
Ko-reh-wa tai-hen foo-roo-ee dess-ka?

What is this place called?
Kono tokoro-wa nan to iimasu-ka?
Ko-no toh-ko-ro-wa nahn toh ee'ee-mahss-ka?

It's magnificent!
Subarashii desu!
Soo-ba-ra-shee'ee dess!

Can one take photographs here?
Koko-de shashin-o toru koto-ga dekimasu-ka?
Ko-ko-deh sha-shin-o toh-roo ko-toh-ga deh-kee-mahss-ka?

You can.	**You cannot.**	**It is forbidden.**
Dekimasu.	Dekimasen.	Kinshi desu.
Deh-kee-mahss.	*Deh-kee-ma-sen.*	*Keen-shee dess.*

Where is a camera shop?
Kamera-ya doko desu-ka?
Ka-meh-ra-ya doh-ko dess-ka?

I would like film.
Fuirumu-ga hoshii desu.
Foo-ee-roo-moo-ga ho-shee'ee dess.

Color.	**White and black.**
Karā.	Shiro-kuro.
Ka-rā.	*Shee-ro-koo-ro.*

Movie film.	**For this camera.**
Eiga-no fuirumu.	Kono kamera-ni.
Eh-ee-ga-no foo-ee-roo-moo.	*Ko-no ka-meh-ra-nee.*

Please develop.
Genzō shite kudasai.
Ghen-zō shee-teh koo-da-sai.

How much is it per print?
Ichi mai ikura desu-ka?
Ee-chee mai ee-koo-ra dess-ka?

Two of each.
Ni mai zutsu.
Nee mai zoo-t'soo.

An enlargement.
Hiki no bashi.
Hee-kee no ba-shee.

This size.
Kono saizu.
Ko-no sa-ee-zoo?

When will they be ready?
Itsu dekimasu-ka?
Eet-soo deh-kee-mahss-ka?

Come back tomorrow.*
Ashita kite kudasai.
Ah-shee-ta kee-teh koo-da-sai.

Can you repair this camera?
Kono kamera-o shūri
   dekimasu-ka?
*Ko-no ka-meh-ra-o shoō-ree
   deh-kee-mahss-ka?*

Yes, we can.
Hai, dekimasu.
Hai, deh-kee-mahss.

May I take a picture of you?
Anata-no shashin-o totte ii desu-ka?
Ah-na-ta-no sha-shin-o toht-teh ee'ee dess-ka?

Stand here, please.
Koko-ni tatte kudasai.
Ko-ko-nee taht-teh koo-da-sai.

Don't move, please.
Ugoka nai de kudasai.
Oo-go-ka nai deh koo-da-sai.

*See page 35 for names of days.

Smile!
Waratte!
Wa-raht-teh!

Good!
Ii desu!
Ee' ee dess!

Will you take one of me, please?
Dōzo, watakushi-o totte kudasai?
Dōh-zo, wa-tahk-shee-o toh-teh koo-da-sai?

In front of this.
Koko-no mae desu.
Ko-ko-no ma-eh dess.

You are very kind.
Goshin setsu-ni.
Go-shin set-soo-nee.

May I send you a copy?
Kopī-o okutte ii desu-ka?
Ko-pēē-o o-koot-teh ee' ee dess-ka?

Your name?
O namae-wa?
O na-ma-eh-wa?

Address?
Jūsho-wa?
Jōō-sho-wa?

12. Entertainment

This section will show you how to extend and accept invitations, as well as suggest things to do. It also offers some typical conversations for theater or nightclubs and some suitable words of appreciation when you are invited for dinner. Remember to name the subject of the invitation *first*, as the dots indicate.

Things to Do

To lunch . . .	To dinner . . .	For a cocktail . . .
Ranchi-ni . . .	Yūshoku-ni . . .	Kakuteru-ni . . .
Rahn-chee-nee . . .	*Yoō-sho-koo-nee* . . .	*Ka-koo-teh-roo-nee* . . .

To the theater . . .	To the movies . . .	For a drive . . .
Gekijō-ni . . .	Ei-ga-ni . . .	Doraibu-ni . . .
Geh-kee-jō-nee . . .	*Ey-ga-nee* . . .	*Drai-boo-nee* . . .

. . . I wish to invite (you).	With pleasure!
. . . shōtai shitai desu.	Yorokonde!
. . . *shō-tai shee-tai dess.*	*Yo-ro-kohn-deh!*

Sorry, I can't.
Sumimasen, dekimasen.
Soo-mee-ma-sen, deh-kee-ma-sen.

I'm busy today.
Kyō-wa isogashii.
K'yō-wa ee-so-ga-shee'ee.

I'm very tired.
Taihen tsukaremashita.
Tai-hen t'soo-ka-reh-mahsh-ta.

I don't feel well.
Kibun-ga yoku nai desu.
Kee-boon-ga yo-koo nai dess.

Perhaps another time.
Tabun tsugi-no kikai-ni.
*Ta-boon t'soo-ghee-no
kee-kai-nee.*

(As for) tennis . . .
Tenis-ga . . .
Ten-iss-ga . . .

Golf . . .
Gorufu-ga . . .
Gor-foo-ga . . .

Dancing . . .
Odori-ga . . .
O-dor-ee-ga . . .

. . . do you like it?
. . . suki desu-ka?
. . . skee dess-ka?

Where are we going tomorrow?
Ashita-wa doko-ni ikimasu-ka?
Ah-shee-ta-wa doh-ko-nee ee-kee-mahss-ka?

. . . to the park.
Kō-en-ni . . .
Kō-en-nee . . .

. . . to the beach.
Kaigan-ni . . .
Kai-gahn-nee . . .

. . . to a department store.
Depāto-ni . . .
Deh-pā-toh-nee . . .

. . . to the shops.
Mise-ni . . .
Mee-seh-nee . . .

. . . to a sushi restaurant.
O-sushi-ya-ni . . .
O-soo-shee-ya-nee . . .

. . . to the sumō wrestling.
Sumō-ni . . .
Soo-mō-nee . . .

. . . to a baseball game.
Beisubōru-no shiai-ni . . .
Beh-soo-bō-roo-no shee-ai-nee . . .

Let's go . . .
. . . ikimashō.
. . . ee-kee-ma-shō.

Note: "Let's go" comes at the end of the sentence, as is the case with other verbs in Japanese.

Theaters and Nightclubs

Let's go to the theater.
Gekijō-ni ikimashō.
Geh-kee-jō-nee ee-kee-mashō.

Two seats, please.
Ni seki-o, kudasai.
Nee seh-kee-o, koo-da-sai.

Who is the star?
Dare-ga shuen?
Da-reh-ga shoo-en?

Beautiful, isn't she?
Utsukushii, desu-ne?
Oots-koo-shee'ee, dess-neh?

When does it start?
Nanji-ni hajimarimasu-ka?
Nahn-jee-nee ha-jee-ma-ree-mahss-ka?

Right away.
Sugu.
Soo-goo.

(In) five minutes.
Go fun (de).
Go foon (deh).

What do you think of it?
Dō omoimasu-ka?
Dōh o-moy-mahss-ka?

It's very good, isn't it?
Taihen ii desu-ne?
Tai-hen ee'ee dess-neh?

It's great!
Subarashii desu!
Soo-ba-ra-shee'ee dess!

It's funny.
Okashīī desu.
O-ka-shee'ee dess.

sad
kanashīī
ka-na-shee'ee

interesting
omoshiroi
o-mo-shee-roy

Is it over?
Owarimashita-ka?
O-wa-ree-mahsh-ta-ka?

Let's go to a nightclub.
Naito kurabu-ni ikimashō.
Nai-toh koo-ra-boo-nee ee-kee-ma-shō.

A table near the dance floor, please.
Dansu furoa-no soba-ni tēburu-o, dōzo.
Dahnss foo-roa-no so-ba-nee tēh-boo-roo-o, dōh-zo.

This one is fine.
Kore-wa ii desu.
Ko-reh-wa ee'ee dess.

Is there a cover charge?
Tēburu chāji-ga arimasu-ka?
*Tēh-boo-roo chā-jee-ga
ah-ree-mahss-ka?*

Shall we dance?
Odorimashō-ka?
O-doh-ree-ma-shō-ka?

You dance very well.
Taihen yoku odorimasu.
*Tai-hen yo-koo o-doh-ree
-mahss.*

Thank you. You too.
Arigatō. Anata mo.
Ah-ree-ga-tōh. Ah-na-ta mo.

It's late, isn't it?
Osoi desu-ne?
Oh-so-ee dess-neh?

That's so. Let's leave.
Sō desu. Demashō.
Sō dess. Deh-ma-shō.

The check, please.
Kanjō-o, kudasai.
Kahn-jō-o, koo-da-sai.

An Invitation to Dinner

Please come to dinner Tuesday evening.
Kayōbi-no yūshoku-ni kite kudasai.
Ka-yō-bee-no yoō-shohk-nee kee-teh koo-da-sai.

With pleasure.
Yorokonde.
Yo-ro-kohn-deh.

Thank you very much.
Dōmo arigatō.
Dōh-mo ah-ree-ga-tōh.

At what time?
Nan ji-ni?
Nahn jee-nee?

At half past eight.
Hachi ji han-ni.
Ha-chee jee hahn-nee.

This is the address.
Kore-wa jūsho desu.
Ko-reh-wa joō-sho dess.

Hand it to the driver.
Untenshu-ni watashite kudasai.
Oon-ten-shoo-nee wa-ta-shee-teh koo-da-sai.

Welcome! Please come in!
Yōkoso! Dōzo ohairi kudasai.
Yō-ko-so! Dōh-zo o-hai-ree koo-da-sai.

I'm sorry I'm late.
Sumimasen okuremashita.
Soo-mee-ma-sen o-koo-reh-mahsh-ta.

The traffic was bad.
Kōtsū-ga warui deshita.
Kō-t'soō-ga wa-roo'ee dehsh-ta.

It doesn't matter.
Kamaimasen.
Ka-mai-ma-sen.

Please make yourself comfortable.
Dōzo o-raku-ni.
Dōh-zo o-ra-koo-nee.

What a beautiful house!
Utsukushii o-uchi desu!
Oot-soo-koo-shee'ee o-oo-chee dess!

This is my wife.	**. . . my son.**	**. . . my daughter.**
Kore wa kanai desu.	. . . musuko.	. . . musume.
	. . . *moo-soo-ko.*	. . . *moo-soo-meh.*
Ko-reh wa ka-nai dess.		

. . . my mother.	**. . . my father.**	**. . . my husband.**
. . . haha.	. . . chichi.	. . . shujin.
. . . *ha-ha.*	. . . *chee-chee.*	. . . *shoo-jeen.*

I am most happy to meet you. (very polite form)
Omeni kakarete ureshii desu.
O-meh-nee ka-ka-reh-teh oo-reh-shee'ee dess.

Omoshiroi (Interesting): It is typical of Japanese politeness that the possessives are not used with family relationships but, instead, special words. When you speak to someone else about *their* family members, use the following honorifics.

your wife	**your mother**	**your father**
oku-san	okā-san	otō-san
your son	**your daughter**	**your husband**
musoko-san	musume-san	go-shujin

The words for "brother" and "sister" are subdivided into words for older and younger sister and brother. (See dictionary starting on page 149).

What will you have to drink?
Nani-o nomimasu-ka?
Na-nee-o no-mee-mahss-ka?

Thank you. Scotch and soda, please.
Arigatō. Skocchi to sōda, dōzo.
Ah-ree-ga-tōh. Sko-chee toh sō-da, dōh-zo.

To your health!	or	**Dry cup!**
Kenkō-no tame-ni!		Kanpai!
Ken-kō-no ta-meh-nee!		*Kahn-pai!*

Dinner is ready.
Yūshuku-ga dekimashita.
Yoō-shoo-koo-ga deh-kee-mahsh-ta.

Please sit here. (on a chair)
Koko-ni o-kake kudasai.
Ko-ko-nee o-ka-keh koo-da-sai.

Please sit here. (on a floor cushion)
Koko-ni o-suwari kudasai.
Ko-ko-nee o-soo-wa-ree koo-da-sai.

The food is delicious!
Tabemono-ga oishii desu!
Ta-beh-mo-no-ga o-ee-shee'ee dess!

Have a little more, please!
Mō sukoshi, dōzo!
Mō sko-shee dōh-zo!

This evening was very enjoyable.
Konbanwa taihen tanoshii deshita.
Kon-bahn-wa tai-hen ta-no-shee'ee desh-ta.

Excuse me.
Sumimasen.
Soo-mee-ma-sen.

Since I have a business meeting in the morning, now I must go.
Asa-ni kaigi-ga, arimasu-node, ima ika nakereba narimasen.
Ah-sa-nee kai-ghee-ga ah-ree-mahss-no-deh, ee-ma ee-ka-na-keh-reh-ba na-ree-ma-sen.

Oh, really?
Ah, so desu-ka?
Ah, so dess-ka?

I'm disappointed.
Zan nen desu.
Zahn nen dess.

However, I under-stand.
Keredomo wakarimasu.
Keh-ree-doh-mo wa-ka-ree-mahss.

Many thanks for your invitation.
Go-shōtai arigatō gozaimasu.
Go-shō-tai ah-ree-ga-tōh go-zai-mahss.

Please come again.
Mata dōzo.
Ma-ta dōh-zo.

Good-bye.
Sayōnara.
Sa-yō-na-ra.

13. Talking to People

Most phrase books are too preoccupied with attending to one's wants and generally "getting along" to pay much attention to what you should say once you meet someone, such as asking people about themselves, their families, and even their opinions about things. Use of the short phrases in this section—both the questions and the answers—can lead to a rewarding conversational breakthrough in Japanese.

Are you living in Tokyo?
Tōkyō-ni sunde imasu-ka?
Tōhk-yō-nee soon-deh ee-mahss-ka?

Where are you from?
Dochira kara desu-ka?
Doh-chee-ra ka-ra dess-ka?

I am from Nara.
Nara-kara desu.
Na-ra-ka-ra dess.

Oh, really?
Ah, sō desu-ka?
Ah, sō dess-ka?

It's a beautiful city.
Utsukushii shi desu.
Oot-soo-koo-shee'ee shee dess.

Have you been in Kobe?
Kōbe-ni ikimashita-ka?
Kō-beh-nee ee-kee-mash-ta-ka?

I haven't been there yet.
Asoko-ni mada ikimasen.
Ah-so-ko-nee ma-da ee-kee-ma-sen.

I would like to go.
Ikitai desu.
Ee-kee-tai dess.

How long are you staying here?
Dono kurai koko-ni taizai desu-ka?
Doh-no koo-rai ko-ko-nee tai-zai dess-ka?

several days
sū nichi
soō nee-chee

several weeks
sū shūkan
soō shoō-kahn

two months
ni-ka getsu
nee-ka get-soo

Have you been in Japan before?
Nihon-ni mae-ni imashita-ka?
Nee-hohn-nee ma-eh-nee ee-mahsh-ta-ka?

Once.
Ichi do.
Ee-chee doh.

Five years ago.
Go nen mae.
Go nen ma-eh.

A long time ago.
Zutto mae.
Zoot-toh ma-eh.

This is my first visit.
Hajimete-no hōmon desu.
Ha-jee-meh-teh-no hō-mohn dess.

Where are you staying?
Doko-ni tomatte imasu-ka?
Doh-ko-nee to-maht-teh ee-mahss-ka?

At which hotel?
Dochira-no hoteru desu-ka?
Doh-chee-ra-no ho-teh-roo dess-ka?

What do you think of Japan?
Nihon-o dō omoimasu-ka?
Nee-hohn-o dōh o-moy-mahss-ka?

I like it very much.
Taihen suki desu.
Tai-hen soo-kee dess.

It is beautiful.
Utsukushii desu.
Oot-soo-koo-shee'ee dess.

Japanese people are charming.
Nihon-no hito-wa miryoku teki desu.
Nee-hohn-no hee-toh-wa mee-r'yo-koo teh-kee dess.

Have you gone to Kyoto?
Kyōto-ni ikimashita-ka?
K'yō-toh-nee ee-kee-mahsh-ta-ka?

Not yet.
Mada desu.
Ma-da dess.

Then you should go.
Sore de wa iku beki desu.
So-reh deh wa ee-koo beh-kee dess.

It is an ancient city.
Furui shi desu.
Foo-roo-ee shee dess.

The temples are magnificent.
Otera-wa subarashii desu.
O-teh-ra-wa soo-ba-ra-shee'ee dess.

Are you from the United States?
Amerika-kara desu-ka?
Ah-meh-ree-ka-ka-ra dess-ka?

That's right.
Sō desu.
Sō dess.

I am from New York.
Niyū Yōku-kara desu.
N'yoō Yohk-ka-ra dess.

I speak only a little Japanese.
Nihon-go-o sukoshi dake hanashimasu.
Nee-hon-go-o s'ko-shee da-keh ha-na-shee-mahss.

I think you speak well.
Jōzu-ni hanasu-to omoimasu.
Jō-zoo-nee ha-na-soo-toh o-moy-mahss.

You are very kind.
Taihen shinsetsu desu.
Tai-hen sheen-set-soo dess.

When people ask your opinion about something or you wish to make a comment, you will find the following phrases helpful.

That's good.
Yoi desu.
Yo'ee dess.

It isn't good.
Yoku nai.
Yo-koo nai.

Very interesting.
Taihen omoshiroi.
Tai-hen o-mo-shee-ro'ee.

Sometimes.   **Often.**   **Not yet.**
Toki doki.   Shiba shiba.   Mada.
Toh-kee doh-kee.   *Shee-ba shee-ba.* *Ma-da.*

That's true.   **That isn't true.**
Honto desu.   Honto de wa arimasen.
Hon-toh dess.   *Hon-to deh wa ah-ree-ma-sen.*

I agree with you.   **Is it possible?**
Dōkan desu.   Dekimasu-ka?
Dōh-kahn dess.   *Deh-kee-mahss-ka?*

I don't know.   **I forget.**
Shirimasen.   Wasuremasu.
Shee-ree-ma-sehn.   *Wa-soo-reh-mahss.*

I remember.
Omoi dashimasu.
O-moy da-shee-mahss.

Are you married?
Kekkon shite imasu-ka?
Kehk-kon shee-teh ee-mahss-ka?

Yes, I am.   **No, I'm not.**
Hai, shite imasu.   Iie, shite imasen.
Hai, shee-teh ee-mahss.   *Ee-yeh, shee-teh ee-ma-sen.*

Is your wife (husband) here?
Oku-san (go shojin)-wa koko-ni imasu-ka?
Ohk-san (go sho-jeen)-wa koko-nee ee-mahss-ka?

Yes, over there.
Hai, asoko-ni.
Hai, ah-so-ko-nee.

He (she) is with some friends.
Kare (kanojo)-wa tomodachi to issho-ni imasu.
*Ka-re (kahn-o-jo)-wa toh-mo-da-chee toh ees-sho-nee
ee-mahss.*

Have you children?
Kodomo-ga arimasu-ka?
*Ko-doh-mo-ga ah-ree-
mahss-ka?*

Yes, we have.
Hai, arimasu.
Hai, ah-ree-mahss.

How many?
Nan-nin?
Nahn-neen?

Boys or girls?
Musuko-san mata-wa
musume-san?
*Moo-soo-ko-san ma-ta-wa
moo-soo-meh-san?*

Boy and girl.
Musuko to musume.
Moo-soo-ko toh moo-soo-meh.

How old are they?
Nan sai desu-ka?
Nahn sa-ee dess-ka?

The boy is five.
Musuko-wa go sai.
Moo-soo-ko-wa go sai.

The girl is ten.
Musume-wa jussai.
Moo-soo-meh-wa joos-sai.

This is a picture of them.
Kore-wa karera-no shashin desu.
Ko-reh-wa ka-reh-ra-no sha-sheen dess.

How charming they are!
Taihen kawaii desu, ne!
Tai-hen ka-wa-ee dess, neh! (The "**ne** is used also for emphasis.)

Do you know that man?
Ano-hito-o shitte imasu-ka?
Ah-no-hee-toh-o sheet-teh ee-mahss-ka?

Do you know that lady?
Ano-josei-o shitte imasu-ka?
Ah-no-jo-seh-ee-o sheet-teh ee-mahss-ka?

Yes. He is a business executive.
Hai. Kare-wa jūyaku desu.
Hai. Ka-reh-wa jōō-ya-koo dess.

. . . a banker.
. . . ginkōka.
. . . ghin-kō-ka.

a lawyer.
bengoshi.
behn-go-shee.

a doctor.
isha.
ees-sha.

a politician.
seijika.
sey-jee-ka.

a movie star.
mūbī sutā.
moō-beē stā.

She is a teacher.
Kanojo-wa sensei desu.
Ka-no-jo-wa sen-seh-ee dess.

an author.
shōsetsuka.
shō-seh-t'soo-ka.

an artist.
gaka.
ga-ka.

an actor (or) actress.
haiyū.
hai-yoō.

Because nouns are neither masuline nor feminine, **haiyū**
can mean actor *or* actress.

He (she) is Japanese.
Nihonjin desu.
Nee-hon-jeen dess.

. . . English.
. . . Eikoku-jin.
. . . Eh-ee-ko-koo-jeen.

. . . American.
. . . Amerika-jin.
. . . Ah-meh-ree-ka-jeen.

Are you Australian?
Anata-wa Ōsutorariya-jin desu-ka?
Ah-na-ta-wa Ō-su-toh-ra-ree-ya-jeen dess-ka?

My wife is French.
Kanai-wa Furansu-jin desu.
Ka-na-ee-wa Foo-rahn-soo-jeen dess.

A German.
Doitsu-jin.
Doh-ee-t'soo-jeen.

Spanish. (person)
Supein-jin.
Soo-peyn-jeen.

A Russian.
Roshiya-jin.
Ro-shee-ya-jeen.

A Chinese.
Chūgoku-jin.
Choō-go-ku-jeen.

Remember that the basic verbs can apply to all pronouns—
I, you, he, she, it, we, and they. Pronouns can be added when
clarification is needed.

What is his occupation?
Shigoto-wa nan desu-ka?
Shee-go-toh-wa nahn dess-ka?

Which country are you from?
Dochira-no kuni-kara desu-ka?
Doh-chee-ra-no koo-nee-ka-ra dess-ka?

Here is (my) card.
Kore-wa meishi desu.
Ko-reh-wa mey-shee dess.

Here is my address in the United States.
Kore-wa watakushi-no Beikoku-no jūsho desu.
Ko-reh-wa wa-tahk-shee-no Bey-ko-koo-no joō-sho dess.

This is the telephone number.
Kore-wa denwa bangō desu.
Ko-reh-wa dehn-wa bahn-gō dess.

When you come to San Francisco, **please telephone.**
San Furansisko-ni kuru-toki, dōzo denwa-o kakete kudasai.
San Fran-sees-ko-nee koo-roo-toh-kee, *dōh-zo, den-wa-o ka-keh-teh koo-da-sai.*

And, on a more personal note:

I enjoyed our meeting.
Ome-ni kakarete ureshii deshita.
O-meh-nee ka-ka-reh-teh oo-reh-shee'ee dehsh-ta.

You are charming.
Anata-wa miryokuteki desu.
Ah-na-ta-wa mee-r'yo-koo-teh-kee dess.

May I call you?
Denwa kakete ii desu-ka?
Dehn-wa ka-keh-teh ee'ee dess-ka?

Tomorrow morning.	**early**	**late**
Ashita-no asa.	hayaku	osoku
Ah-shee-ta-no ah-sa.	*ha-ya-koo*	*oh-so-koo*

Can we meet again?
Mata oai dekimasu-ka?
Ma-ta o-ah-ee deh-kee-mahss-ka?

When?
Itsu-ni?
Ee-t'soo-nee?

Where?
Doko-ni?
Doh-ko-nee?

What's the matter?
Dō shimashita-ka?
Dōh shee-mahsh-ta-ka?

Are you angry?
Okorimasu-ka?
O-ko-ree-mahss-ka?

Why?
Dōshite?
Dōh-shee-teh?

Where are you going?
Doko-ni ikimasu-ka?
Doh-ko-nee ee-kee-mahss-ka?

Let's go together.
Issho-ni ikimashō.
Ees-sho-nee ee-kee-ma-shō.

You are very beautiful.
Taihen utsukushii desu.
Tai-hen oot-soo-koo-shee'ee dess.

graceful
yūbi na
yoō-bee na

intelligent
rikō na
ree-kō na

This is a present for you.
Anata-ni okurimono desu.
Ah-na-ta-nee o-koo-ree-mo-no dess.

Will you give me your picture?
Anata-no shashin-o watakushi-ni kudasaimasu-ka?
*A-na-ta-no sha-sheen-oh wa-tahk-shee-nee koo-da-
   sai-mahss-ka?*

Don't forget!
Wasure nai!
Wa-soo-reh nai!

I like you very much.
Anata-ga taihen sukidesu.
Ah-na-ta-ga tai-hen soo-kee-dess.

Is that true?
Honto desu-ka?
Hohn-toh dess-ka?

Of course.
Mochiron.
Mo-chee-rohn.

Do you like me too?
Anata-mo watakushi-o sukidesu-ka?
Ah-na-ta-mo wa-tahk-shee-o soo-kee-dess-ka?

A Choice of Conversational Expressions

There are certain words that Japanese people use constantly which do not always have an equivalent in English. Used at the right time they will give the impression that, for a visitor, you have a commendable foundation in Japanese culture and speech patterns. The Japanese is given first, just as you will hear these expressions occur in everyday conversations.

Yoi tabi-o, dōzo.
Yoy ta-bee-o, dōh-zo.
Have a good trip.

Tanoshin de kudasai!
Ta-no-sheen deh koo-da-sai!
Enjoy yourself!

Kōun-o inorimasu!
Kō-oon-o in-or-ee-mahss!
Good luck!

Sugu mata kite kudasai!
Soo-goo ma-ta keet-teh
   koo-da-sai!
Come back soon!

When greeting a guest:

Irasshai!
Ee-ra-shai!
Welcome!

When being served by the host, one says:

Itadakimasu.
Ee-ta-da-kee-mahss.
Honorably receive.

After finishing a good meal:

Gochisō-sama!
Go-chee-sō-sa-ma!
Honorably delicious spread!

For making room or pushing past others:

Gomen nasai.
Go-men na-sai.
I'm sorry.

Osaki-ni, dōzo!
O-sa-kee-nee, dōh-zo!
You first, please!

To a visitor to one's home:

Oraku-ni dōzo!
O-ra-koo-nee dōh-zo!
Please relax!

For congratulating someone on birthdays, attainments, honors, or festive occasions:

Omedetō!
O-meh-deh-tōh!
Congratulations!

And, to punctuate conversations:

Mochiron!	**Anō . . . .**
Mo-chee-rohn!	Ah-nō . . .
Of course!	*Well, then (or) so . . .*

Ah, sō desu-ka?	**Sō desu.**	**Sō desu-ne?**
Ah, sō dess-ka?	Sō dess.	Sō dess-neh?
Oh, is that so?	*That's so.*	*That's so, isn't it?*

Iie, sō de wa arimasen.
Ee-yeh, sō deh wa ah-ree-ma-sen.
No, it isn't so.

Sono-go ikaga desu-ka?
So-no-go ee-ka-ga dess-ka?
How have you been?

Mā, mā desu.
Mā, mā dess.
So so.

Subarashii!
Soo-ba-ra-shee'ee!
Great!

Yoku nai.
Yo-koo nai.
Not so good.

Nan desu-ka?
Nahn dess-ka?
What's going on?

Dō deshita-ka?
Dōh desh-ta-ka?
What happened?

Kawatte imasu ne!
Ka-wa-teh ee-mahss neh!
How unusual!

Nan de mo nai.
Nahn deh mo nai.
Nothing at all.

Shikata nai.
Shee-ka-ta nai.
It can't be helped.

Kamaimasen.
Ka-mai-ma-sen.
It doesn't matter.

Goshinpai nai!
Go-sheen-pai nai!
Don't worry!

Mō ichi do, dōzo.
Mō ee-chee doh, dōh-zo.
Once again, please.

Nan-to iimashita-ka?
Nahn-toh ee'ee-mahsh-ta ka?
What did you say?

Dekimasu-ka?
Deh-kee-mahss-ka?
Is it possible?

Yasashii desu.
Ya-sa-shee'ee dess.
It's easy.

Muzukashii.
Moo-zoo-ka-shee'ee.
Difficult.

Fukanō.
Foo-ka-nō.
Impossible.

Kinshi.
Keen-shee.
Forbidden.

An expression of surprise or mild expletive you will frequently hear varies according to the sex of the speaker.

A man will say: **Wā! Sugoi na!**
                 Wā! Soo-goy na!

A woman will say: **Mā! Sugoi-wa-ne!**
                  Mā! Soo-goy-wa-neh!

You will frequently hear or need to use one of the following expressions to attract attention.

Ano-ne!
Ah-no-neh!
Say there!

Moshi, moshi!
Mo-shee, mo-shee!
Hello, hello!

Chotto, chotto!
Cho-toh, cho-toh!
Moment, moment!

14: Shopping

Wasure nai! (Don't forget!): Always put the shop or place you are looking for first, add **-wa**, and then say **doko desu-ka** ("Where is it?")

Also, the names of shops are usually formed by adding **-ya** to the product sold there.

Names of Shops

Where is there a bookstore?
Honya-wa doko desu-ka?
Hon-ya-wa doh-ko dess-ka?

Where is there a jewelry store?
Hōseki-ya-wa doko-desu-ka?
Hō-seh-kee-ya-wa doh-ko dess-ka?

a perfume shop
kōsui-ya
kō-soo-ee-ya

a flower shop
hana-ya
ha-na-ya

a toy shop
omocha-ya
o-mo-cha-ya

a camera shop
kamera-ya
ka-meh-ra-ya

a barber shop
sanpatsu-ya
sahn-pat-soo-ya

a beauty shop
biyōin
bee-yō-een

a food market
māketto
mā-keht-toh

a drugstore (pharmacy)
yakkyoku
yahk-ky-o-koo

a department store	**men's section, please**	**ladies section, please**
depāto	shinshi mono, dōzo	fujin mono, dōzo
deh-pā-to	*sheen-shee mo-no, dōh-zo*	*foo-jeen mo-no, dōh-zo*

General Shopping Vocabulary

Welcome!
Irasshai!
Eer-ra-shai!

May I help you?
Nanika shimashō-ka?
Na-nee-ka shee-ma-shō-ka?

Excuse me, I'm just looking.
Sumimasen, miru dake desu.
Soo-mee-ma-sen, mee-roo da-keh dess.

Thank you.
Arigatō.
Ah-ree-ga-tōh.

I'll be back later.
Ato-de kimasu.
Ah-toh-deh kee-mahss.

I want to buy a present	**for my wife**	**for my husband**
Purezento-o kaitai desu	kanai-ni	shujin-ni
Preh-zento-o kai-tai dess	*ka-nai-nee*	*shoo-jin-nee*

something for a man
otoko-no mono
o-toh-ko-no mo-no

something for a lady
fujin-no mono
foo-jeen-no mo-no

I like this.
Kore-ga sukidesu.
Ko-reh-ga soo-kee-dess.

How much is it?
Ikura desu-ka?
Ee-koo-ra dess-ka?

Please show me another.
Hokano-o misete kudasai.
Ho-ka-no-o mee-seh-teh koo-da-sai.

Something less expensive.
Mō sukoshi yasui mono.
Mō sko-shee ya-soo-ee mo-no.

Do you like this one?
Kore-o sukidesu-ka?
Ko-reh-o soo-keh-dess-ka.

May I try it on?
Kite mite ii desu-ka?
Kee-teh mee-teh ee'ee dess-ka?

Does it fit well?
Chōdo aimasu-ka?
Chō-doh ai-mahss-ka?

Can you alter it?
Naoshi-ga dekimasu-ka?
Na'oh-shee-ga deh-kee-mahss-ka?

What day will it be ready?
Nan-nichi-ni dekimasu-ka?
Nahn-nee-chee-nee deh-kee-mahss-ka?

Good! I'll buy it.
Yoroshii! Kore-o kaimasu.
Yo-ro-shee'ee! Ko-reh-o kai-mahss.

I'll take it with me.
Motte kaerimasu.
Mo-teh ka-eh-ree-mahss.

Please send it to this address.
Kono jūsho-ni okutte kudasai.
Ko-no joō-sho-nee o-koot-teh koo-da-sai.

Is a credit card o.k.?
Kurejitto kādo ii desu-ka?
Koo-reh-jeet-toh kā-doh ee'ee dess-ka?

Of course. Sign, please.
Mochiron. Shomei shite, kudasai.
Mo-chee-ron. Sho-mey shee-teh, koo-da-sai.

I'll pay cash.
Genkin-de haraimasu.
Gen-keen-deh ha-rai-mahss.

My change, please.
Otsuri-o, kudasai.
O-t'soo-ree-o, koo-da-sai.

Clothes

blouse	**skirt**	**suit (male or female)**
braus	skāto	sūtsu
boo-ra-o-soo	*skā-toh*	*soō-t'soo*

coat	**hat**	**scarf**
kōto	bōshi	skāfu
kō-toh	*bō-shee*	*skāf*

handbag	gloves	handkerchiefs
hando bakku	tebukuro	hankachi
hahn-doh bahk-koo	*teh-boo-koo-ro*	*hahn-ka-chee*

dress	shirt	pants
doresu	waishatsu	zubon
doh-reh-soo	*wai-sha-t' soo*	*zoo-bon*

jacket	tie	socks
uwagi	nekutai	sokkusu
oo-wa-jee	*nek-tai*	*soks-soo*

undershirt	undershorts
shitagi	pantsu
shee-ta-ghee	*pants*

stockings	slip	brassiere
stokkingu	shimiizu	burajyā
stok-king	*shee-mēē'eez*	*boo-ra-jyā*

panties	nightgown
pantee	naitogaun
pan-tee	*nait-gown*

towel	bathrobe	swimsuit
tenugui	basurōpu	kaisuigi
ten-gwee	*ba-soo-rō-poo*	*kai-swee-ghee*

Visitors to Japan may wish to purchase examples of traditional Japanese clothing such as:

kimono (for women)	kimono (for men)
fujin-no kimono	otoko-no kimono
foo-jeen-no kee-mo-no	*o-toh-ko-no kee-mo-no*

(cotton kimono)
yukata
yoo-ka-ta

(thonged sandals)
zōri
zō-ree

(wooden clogs)
geta
geh-ta

(slipper socks)
tabi
ta-bee

Sizes—Colors—Materials

What size?
Saizu-wa nan desu-ka?
Sai-zoo-wa nahn dess-ka?

small	**medium**	**large**	**extra large**
chiisai	chū gurai	ōkii	tokudai
chee'ee-sai	*choō goo-rai*	*ō-kee'ee*	*toh-koo-dai*

larger	**smaller**	**wider**
motto okii	motto chiisai	motto hiroi
moht-toh o-kee'ee	*moht-toh chee'ee-sai*	*moht-toh hee-roy*

narrower	**longer**	**shorter**
motto semai	motto nagai	motto mijikai
moht-toh seh-mai	*moht-toh na-gai*	*moht-toh mee-jee-kai*

What color?	**red**	**blue**	**yellow**
Nani iro?	akai	aoi	ki iro
Na-nee ee-ro?	*ah-kai*	*ah-oy*	*kee ee-ro*

orange
orenji
o-ren-jee

green
midori iro
mee-doh-ree ee-ro

purple
murasaki
moo-ra-sa-kee

gray
nezumi iro
neh-zoo-mee ee-ro

brown
cha iro
cha ee-ro

black
kuro
koo-ro

white
shiro
shee-ro

darker
motto koi
moh-toh ko-ee

lighter
motto usui
moht-toh oo-swee

Is it silk?
Kinu desu-ka?
Kee-noo dess-ka?

linen
asa
ah-sa

wool
uūru
oo-oo-roo

cotton
momen
mo-men

lace
leisu
lace

nylon
nairon
nai-rohn

polyester
poriesuta
po-ree-ess-ta

leather
kawa
ka-wa

suede
suēdo
swēh-doh

plastic
purasuchikku
p'rahs-cheek-koo

What kind of fur is this?
Kore-wa nani-no kegawa desu-ka?
Ko-reh-wa na-nee-no keh-ga-wa dess-ka?

fox	beaver	mink
kitsune	bīva	minku
keet-soo-neh	*beē-va*	*meen-ku*

chinchilla	leopard	rabbit
chinchira	hyō	usagi
cheen-chee-la	*h'yō*	*oo-sa-ghee*

Newsstand

---

magazine(s)	newspaper(s)	postcards
zasshi	shinbun	hagaki
zahs-shee	*sheen-boon*	*ha-ga-kee*

a map of the city	a guide book	in English, please
shi-no chizu	gaido bukku	eigo-de dōzo
shee-no chee-zoo	*gai-doh boo-koo*	*ey-go-deh dōh-zo*

Drugstore

---

toothbrush	toothpaste
haburashi	hamigaki
ha-boo-ra-shee	*ha-mee-ga-kee*

razor	shaving cream
kamisori	higesori-no kurīmu
ka-mee-soo-ree	*hee-gheh-sa-ree-no krē̄-moo*

lotion
rōshiyon
rō-shon

electric razor
denki kamisori
den-kee ka-mee-soo-ree

hairbrush
kami burashi
ka-mee boo-ra-shee

comb
kushi
koo-shee

aspirin
asupirin
ah-soo-pee-reen

antiseptic
shōdoku eki
shō-doh-koo eh-kee

scissors
hasami
ha-sa-mee

nail file
tsume migaki
t'soo-meh mee-ga-kee

plastic bandage
bansōkō
bahn-sō-kō

sunglasses
sangurasu
sahn-goo-ra-soo

cigarettes
shigaretto (or) tabako
shee-ga-ret-toh (or) ta-ba-ko

matches
matchi
maht-chee

cigar
hamaki
ha-ma-kee

pipe
paipu
pai-poo

Have you American cigarettes?
Amerika-no shigaretto-ga arimasu-ka?
Ah-meh-ree-ka-no shee-ga-ret-toh-ga ah-ree-mahss-ka?

cough drops
seki dome
seh-kee doh-meh

Cosmetics

powder	lipstick	eye shadow
kona	kuchibeni	aishadō
ko-na	*koo-chee-beh-nee*	*ah-ee-sha-dōh*

nail polish	eyebrow pencil
manikyua eki	mayuzumi
ma-nee-k'yoo-ah eh-ki	*ma-yoo-zoo-mee*

cleanser	cotton	hair spray
kurenzā kurīimu	wata	kami-no supurei
kren-zā koo-ree-moo	*wa-ta*	*ka-mee-no spray*

shampoo	perfume
shampū	kōsui
shahm-pōo	*kō-swee*

It's a pleasant fragrance, isn't it?
Ii nioi, desu-ne?
Ee' ee nee-oy, dess-neh?

I want my hair washed . . .   and set.
Kami-o araitai desu . . .   sore-to setto.
Ka-mee-o ah-rai-tai dess . . .   so-reh-toh seht-toh.

a tint	a little lighter	a little darker
kezome	mō sukoshi usui	mō sukoshi koi
keh-zo-meh	*mō sko-shee oo-swee*	*mō sko-shee ko-ee*

the same color	a permanent	a manicure
onaji iro	pāmanento	manikyua
oh-na-jee ee-ro	*pā-ma-nen-toh*	*ma-nee-k'yoo-ah*

Barber

shave
higesori
hee-gheh-so-ree

haircut
sanpatsu
sahn-pat-soo

massage
massaji
ma-sā-jee

Use scissors, please.
Hasami-de, dōzo.
Ha-sa-mee-deh, dōh-zo.

shorter
motto mijikaku
moht-toh mee-jee-ka-koo

not too short
amari mijikaku nai
ah-ma-ree mee-jee-ka-koo nai.

on top
ue-ni
oo-eh-nee

in back
ushiro-ni
oo-shee-ro-nee

on the sides
waki-ni
wa-kee-nee

Is that o.k.?
Ii desu-ka?
Ee'ee dess-ka?

That's fine!
Yoroshii.
Yo-ro-shee'ee!

Food Market

Weight is measured by kilo, approximately 2.2 pounds.
Counts of ten are used instead of dozens.

Please, I want five of these.
Dōzo, kore-o itsutsu hoshii desu.
Dōh-zo, ko-reh-o ee-t'soo-t'soo ho-shee'ee dess.

Ten of those also, please.
Sore-o tō, dōzo.
So-reh-o tōh, dōh-zo.

Three cans of this, please.
Kono kan-o mittsu, kudasai.
Ko-no kahn-o meet-t'soo, koo-da-sai.

Is this fresh?
Atarashii desu-ka?
Ah-ta-ra-shee'ee dess-ka?

How much per kilo?
Ichi kiro ikura desu-ka?
Ee-chee kee-ro ee-koo-ra dess-ka?

Can one buy sake here?	**wine**	**mineral water**
Sake-o koko-de kaemasu-ka?	budōshu	tansan-sui
Sa-keh-o ko-ko-deh ka-eh-mahss-ka?	*boo-dōh-shoo*	*tahn-sahn-swee*

Put it in a bag, please.
Dōzo, fukuro-ni irete kudasai.
Dōh-zo, foo-koo-ro-nee ee-reh-teh koo-da-sai.

Jewelry

Please show me some rings.
Yubiwa-o misete kudasai.
Yoo-bee-wa-o mee-seh-teh koo-da-sai.

How much is this ring?
Kono yubiwa-wa ikura desu-ka?
Ko-no yoo-bee-wa-wa ee-koo-ra dess-ka?

watch	necklace	bracelet	earrings
tokei	nekkuresu	udewa	mimikazari
toh-keh'ee	*nek-kress*	*oo-deh-wa*	*mee-mee-ka-zah-ree*

Is this gold . . . or gold plated   **platinum**   **silver**

Kin desu-ka? . . . mata-wa kin   purachina   gin
                          mekki   *poo-ra-chee-na*   *gheen*

Keen dess-ka? . . . ma-ta-wa keen
                          meh-kee

pearls	black pearls	pink pearls
shinju	kuro shinju	pinku shinju
sheen-joo	*koo-ro sheen-joo*	*pin-koo sheen-joo*

diamond   **ruby**
daiyamondo   rubī
dai-ya-mon-do   *roo-bēē*

sapphire	emerald	jade
safaiya	emerarudo	hisui
sa-fai-ya	*eh-meh-ra-roo-doh*	*hee-swee*

Where does this jade come from?
Kono hisui-wa doko-kara desu-ka?
Ko-no hee-swee-wa doh-ko-ka-ra dess-ka?

Antiques

Is it very old?
Kore-wa taihen furui desu-ka?
Ko-reh-wa tai-hen foo-roo-ee dess-ka?

It's really beautiful!
Taihen utsukushii desu-ne!
Taihen oot-soo-koo-shee'ee dess-neh!

What period is it from?
Itsu-no jidai desu-ka?
Ee-t'soo-no jee-dai dess-ka?

Is it very expensive?
Taihen takai desu-ka?
Tai-hen ta-kai dess-ka?

Is it an antique?	**woodprint**	**carving**
Jidai mono?	hanga	horimono
Jee-dai mo-no?	*hahn-ga*	*ho-ree-mo-no*

furniture	**a painting**	**a screen**
kagu	e	byōbu
ka-goo	*eh*	*b'yō-boo*

a doll	**a sword**
ningyō	katana
ning-yō	*ka-ta-na*

Can you ship it?	**to this address**
Okuru koto-ga dekimasu-ka?	kono jūsho-ni
O-koo-roo ko-toh-ga deh-kee-mahss-ka?	*ko-no jōō-sho-nee*

to America	**to England**	**to Canada**
Amerika-ni	Eikoku-ni	Kanada-ni
Ah-meh-ree-ka-nee	*Eh-ee-ko-koo-nee*	*Ka-na-da-nee*

How much are the shipping charges?
Funachin-wa ikura desu-ka?
Foo-na-cheen-wa ee-koo-ra dess-ka?

When will it arrive?
Itsu tsukimasu-ka?
Eet-soo t'soo-kee-mahss-ka?

15. Telephone

Talking on the telephone is an excellent test of your ability to communicate in Japanese because you can't see the person you are talking to or use gestures to help get your meaning across. When asking for someone, simply say his or her name, followed by **san,** then **o**, and then **dōzo**. You will not have to say the individual numbers because the direct dial system is in general use in Japan.

Where is the telephone?
Denwa-wa doko desu-ka?
Den-wa-wa doh-ko dess-ka?

Where is a public telephone?
Kōshū denwa doko desu-ka?
Kō-shoō den-wa doh-ko dess-ka?

How much do I put in?
Ikura iremasu-ka?
Ee-koo-ra ee-reh-mahss-ka?

A ten yen coin.
Jū en dama.
Joō en da-ma.

Hello!
Moshi moshi!
Mo-shee mo-shee!

Information, please.
Denwa annai, dōzo.
Den-wa ahn-nai, dōh-zo.

Are you the hotel operator?
Hoteru-no kōkanshu, desu-ka?
Ho-teh-roo-no kō-kan-shoo, dess-ka?

Please, number 756-6301.
Dōzo, denwa bango-wa shichi gō roku-roku san rei ichi.
Dōh-zo, den-wa bahn-go-wa shee-chee go ro-koo-ro-koo sahn rey ee-chee.

Do you speak English?
Eigo-o hanashimasu-ka?
Eh-go-o ha-na-shee-mahss-ka?

Person to person.
Shimei denwa.
Shee-meh'ee den-wa.

Collect call.
Senpō barai.
Sen-pō ba-rai.

I want to call America.
Amerika-ni kaketai desu.
Ah-meh-ree-ka-nee ka-keh-tai dess.

Number 305-896-7231.
Bangō san rei gō-hachi ku roku-shichi ni san ichi.
*Bahn-gō sahn rey gō-ha-chee koo ro-koo-shee-chee nee sahn
ee-chee.*

Hold the line, please.
Kono mana, dōzo.
Ko-no ma-na, dōh-zo.

The line is busy.
Hanashichū desu.
Ha-na-shee-choō dess.

Please call again.
Mō ichi do kakete kudasai.
Mō ee-chee doh ka-keh-teh koo-da-sai.

Sorry, wrong number.
Sumimasen machigai, desu.
Soo-mee-ma-sen ma-chee-gai, dess.

Mr. Sugimura, please.
Sugimura-san-o, dōzo.
Soo-ghee-moo-ra-sahn-o, dōh-zo.

He's not there?
Imasen-ka?
Ee-ma-sen-ka?

When is he coming back?
Itsu kaerimasu-ka?
Eet-soo ka-eh-ree-mahss-ka?

Please repeat.
Mō ichi do itte kudasai.
Mo ee-chee doh ee-teh koo-da-sai.

At three o'clock.
San ji-ni.
Sahn jee-nee.

Very well, I'll call back.
Yoroshii, mō ichi do kakemasu.
Yo-ro-shee'ee, mō ee-chee doh ka-keh-mahss.

Who is calling?
Donata desu-ka?
Doh-no-ta dess-ka?

Please take a message.
Messēji-o shite kudasai.
Mess-sēh-jee-o shee-teh koo-da-sai.

My name is . . .
Watakushi-no namae-wa . . . desu.
Wa-tahk-shee-no na-ma-eh-wa . . . dess.

My number is . . .
Watakushi-no bangō-wa . . . desu.
Wa-tahk-shee-no bahn-gō-wa . . . dess.

Annai (Information): Besides their graceful and often compli-
cated ideograms the Japanese have a set of alphabetical syllables, useful in spelling foreign words and names. Therefore,
if you tell someone your name, say it in distinct syllables, so
a Japanese who takes the message can write it in this special
syllable writing if he or she does not write English.

The sounds of these seventy-six signs are written in English letters on the second line of each phrase in this book.
The Japanese call the system of writing in our Roman alphabet **roma-ji**—literally "Roman letters."

You will find these syllable signs written in Japanese on page 123.

And, if there is no coin telephone available:

May I use your phone?
Denwa-o okari dekimasu-ka?
Den-wa-o o-ka-ree deh-kee-mahss-ka?

It is a local call.
Shinai denwa desu.
Shee-nai den-wa dess.

Certainly, go ahead.
Mochiron, dōzo.
Mo-chee-ron, dōh-zo.

Thank you very much.
Dōmo arigatō.
Dōh-mo ah-ree-ga-tōh.

Excuse me, how much is the call?
Sumimasen, denwa dai-wa ikura?
Soo-mee-ma-sen, den-wa dai-wa ee-koo-ra?

There is no charge.
Tada desu.
Ta-da dess.

16. Post Office—Letters—Telegrams—Cables

郵便局

One of the first things one does when abroad is to write postcards—**hagaki**—to friends and relatives. You might also impress your friends by adding a few words in Japanese, which you will find on page 125.

Are there letters for me?
Watakushi-ni tegami-ga arimasu-ka?
Wa-ta-koo-shee-nee teh-ga-mee-ga ah-ree-mahss-ka?

I need writing paper.
Binsen-ga hitsuyō desu.
Been-sen-ga hit-soo-yō dess.

envelopes	postcards	pen
fūtō	hagaki	pen
foo-tōh	*ha-ga-kee*	*pen*

pencil	stamps
enpitsu	kitte
en-pee-t'soo	*keet-teh*

Where is the post office?
Yūbin kyoku-wa doko desu-ka?
Yoō-been kyo-koo-wa doh-ko dess-ka?

How much is airmail to America?
Kōkū bin Amerika-made ikura desu-ka?
Kō-koō been Ah-meh-ree-ka-ma-deh ee-koo-ra dess-ka?

to Canada?
Kanada-made?
Ka-na-da-ma-deh?

to England?
Eikoku-made?
Ey-ko-ku-ma-deh?

to Australia?
Ōsutoraria-made?
Ō-soo-toh-ra-ree-ah-ma-deh?

registered letter
kakitome-yūbin
ka-kee-tōh-mee-yoō-bin

insured letter
hoken-yūbin
ho-ken-yoō-bin

Where is the telegraph office?
Denpō kyoku doko desu-ka?
Den-pō k'yo-koo doh-ko dess-ka?

cable
denshin
den-shin

telegram
denpō
den-pō

How much per word?
Ichi-ji ikura desu-ka?
Ee-chee-jee ee-koo-ra dess-ka?

How to Write Your Name and Read Simple Signs

Japanese is partially written with Chinese characters, usually mixed with one of the two principal sound alphabets that the

Japanese have developed. One of these sound alphabets or, more precisely, "syllable" alphabets, is relatively easy to write and read and is recognizable by its simple straight lines. It is called Katakana and is often used on signs and in writing foreign names. Here is the Katakana alphabet of syllable sounds followed by the Roman script (**Roma-ji**) used by the Japanese. Because Japanese does not have the sound of the English "L", the "R" sound is used as an approximation.

ア a	イ i	ウ u	エ e	オ o
カ ka	キ ki	ク ku	ケ ke	コ ko
ガ ga	ギ gi	グ gu	ゲ ge	ゴ go
サ sa	シ shi	ス su	セ se	ソ so
ザ za	ジ zi	ズ zu	ゼ ze	ゾ zo
タ ta	チ tchi	ツ tsu	テ te	ト to
ダ da	ヂ dji	ヅ dsu	デ de	ド do
ナ na	ニ ni	ヌ nu	ネ ne	ノ no
ハ ha	ヒ hi	フ fu	ヘ he	ホ ho
バ ba	ビ bi	ブ bu	ベ be	ボ bo
パ pa	ピ pi	プ pu	ペ pe	ポ po
マ ma	ミ mi	ム mu	メ me	モ mo

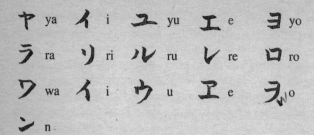

ヤ ya　イ i　ユ yu　エ e　ヨ yo
ラ ra　リ ri　ル ru　レ re　ロ ro
ワ wa　イ i　ウ u　エ e　ヲ wo
ン n

Some of the signs that you may see in Japan will be written in Katakana as follows:

Hotel

ホ テ ル

Hoteru

Bar

バ ー

Bā-ā

Taxi

タ ク シ ー

Takushī

Restaurant

レ ス ト ラ ン

Restoran

To see how your own name would look in Japanese, choose the individual syllables that correspond to its sound:

Baker

ベ ー カ ー

Bēkā

Smith

ス ミ ス

Sumisu

Mac Donald

マ ク ド ナ ル ド

Maku Donarudo

Tom

ト ム

Tomu

Dick

デ イ ツ ク

Dikku

Harry

ハ リ ー

Harī

In the above, the long sign "-", which we have used throughout the book, *follows* the vowel when written in Katakana.

To illustrate how Japanese words can be written in the Katakana script (and **Roma-ji**), observe the following "postcard" phrases, parts of which you might copy for your own informal correspondence, substituting the name of the person to whom you are writing for the feminine Japanese name **Aiko**.

Dear Aiko,	**How are you?**
アイコサマ	イカガデスカ？
Aiko-sama,	Ikaga desu-ka?

I am in Nara.

ナラニイマス

Nara-ni imasu.

It is very beautiful.

タイヘンキレイデス

Taihen kirei-desu.

If you were here, it would be better.

モシ アナタガ イレバ モットイイデス

Moshi anata-ga ireba motto ii desu.

Greetings to everyone.

ミナサマニ ヨロシク

Mina sama-ni yoroshiku.

Till soon.

デ ワ マ タ

De wa mata.

Good-bye.

サ ヨ ウ ナ ラ

Sayonara.

17: Seasons and the Weather

winter
fuyu
foo-yoo

spring
haru
ha-roo

summer
natsu
naht-soo

autumn
aki
ah-kee

How is the weather?
Otenki-wa dō desu-ka?
O-ten-kee-wa dōh dess-ka?

The weather is fine.
Ii otenki desu.
Ee'ee o-ten-kee dess.

It's very hot, isn't it?
Taihen atsui desu, ne?
Tai-hen aht-soo'ee dess, neh?

Let's swim.
Oyogi mashō.
O-yo-ghee ma-shō.

Where's the pool?
Pūru-wa doko desu-ka?
Poō-roo-wa doh-ko dess-ka?

It's raining.
Ame-ga futte imasu.
Ah-meh-ga foo-teh ee-mahss.

I need an umbrella.	**boots**	**a raincoat**
Kasa-ga hitsuyō desu.	naga gutsu	reinkōto
Ka-sa-ga heet-soo-yō dess.	*na-ga goot-soo*	*rein-kō-toh*

It's snowing.
Yuki-ga futte imasu.
Yoo-kee-ga foo-teh ee-mahss.

It's windy.
Kaze-ga fuite imasu.
Ka-zeh-ga foo'ee-teh ee-mahss.

It's cold.
Samui desu.
Sa-moo'ee dess.

Do you like to ski?
Sukīī-ga sukidesu-ka?
Soo-keē'ee-ga soo-kee-dess-ka?

I want to rent skis.
Sukīī-o karitai desu.
Soo-keē'ee-o ka-ree-tai dess.

18. Doctor

I am ill.
Byōki desu.
B'yō-kee dess.

I need a doctor.
Isha ga hitsuyō desu.
Ee-sha ga heet-soo-yō dess.

It's urgent.
Jūyō desu.
Joō-yō dess.

It's an emergency.
Kinkyū desu.
Keen-k'yoō dess.

Can he come right away?
Kare-wa sugu kuru koto-ga dekimasu-ka?
Ka-reh-wa soo-goo koo-roo ko-toh-ga deh-kee-mahss-ka?

Well, what's wrong with you?
Sō, dō shimashita-ka?
Sō, dōh shee-mahsh-ta-ka?

I don't feel well.
Kibun-ga yokunai desu.
Kee-boon-ga yo-koo-nai dess.

Where does it hurt?
Doko-ga itai desu-ka?
Doh-ko-ga ee-tai dess-ka?

Here.
Koko.
Ko-ko.

129

My head hurts.
Atama-ga itai desu.
Ah-ta-ma-ga ee-tai dess.

throat
nodo
no-do

ear
mimi
mee-mee

stomach
onaka
o-na-ka

back
senaka
seh-na-ka

I hurt my leg.
Ashi-o itamemashita.
*Ah-shee-o ee-ta-meh-ma-
    shee-ta.*

ankle
ashi kubi
ah-shee-koo-bee

knee
hiza
hee-za

foot
ashi
ah-shee

arm
ude
oo-deh

hand
te
teh

elbow
hiji
hee-jee

I am dizzy.
Memai-ga suru.
Meh-mai-ga soo-roo.

I have a fever.
Netsu-ga arimasu.
Neht-soo-ga ah-ree-mahss.

I don't sleep.
Nemuremasen.
Neh-moo-reh ma-sen.

I have diarrhea
Geri-o shite imasu.
Geh-ree-o shee-teh ee-mahss.

Since when?
Itsu kara?
Eet-soo ka-ra?

Since yesterday.
Kinō kara.
Kee-nō ka-ra.

Since several days.
Sū nichi mae kara.
Soō nee-chee mah-ee ka-ra.

What have you eaten?
Nani-o tabemashita-ka?
Na-nee-o ta-beh-mahsh-ta-ka?

Undress, please.
Nui-de, kudasai.
Noo-ee-deh, koo-da-sai.

Lie down!
Nete!
Neh-teh!

Stand up!
Tatte!
Ta-teh!

Breathe deeply.
Iki-o foo-kaku.
Ee-kee-o foo-ka-koo.

Open your mouth.
Kuchi-o akete.
Koo-chee-o ah-keh-teh.

Put out your tongue.
Shita-o dashite.
Shee-ta-o da-shee-teh.

Cough.
Seki.
Seh-kee.

Get dressed, please.
Yōfuku-o kite, kudasai.
Yō-foo-koo-o kee-teh, koo-da-sai.

Is it serious?
Taihen warui desu-ka?
Tai-hen wa-roo-ee dess-ka?

Don't worry.
Shinpai nai.
Sheen-pai nai.

It's not that bad.
Sonnani waruku nai
So-na-nee wa-roo-koo nai.

It's indigestion.   **A cold.**
Shōka furyō.   Kaze.
Shō-ka foo-r'yō.   *Ka-zeh.*

A virus.
Densenbyō.
Den-sen-b'yō.

You must stay in bed.
Yoko-ni natte nakereba
  narimasen.
Yo-ko-nee naht-teh na-keh-
  reh-ba na-ree-ma-sen.

Please rest.
Yasunde kudasai.
Ya-soon-deh koo-da-sai.

Take this medication.
Kono kusuri-o nominasai.
Ko-no koo-soo-ree-o no-mee-na-sai.

Be careful, please.
Kiotsukete, kudasai.
K'yo-t'soo-keh-teh, koo-da-sai.

Don't eat too much.
Takusan tabete-wa ikimasen.
Takh-san ta-beh-teh-wa
  ee-kee-ma-sen.

**You should not drink sake
  (alcohol).**
Osake-o noma nai-de.
O-sa-keh-o no-meh nai-deh.

The liver is bad.
Kanzō-ga warui desu.
Kahn-zō-ga wa-roo-ee dess.

It's appendicitis.
Mōchōen desu.
Mō-chō-en dess.

A heart attack.
Shinzō mahi.
Sheen-zō ma-hee.

You need to go to the hospital.
Byōin-ni iku hitsuyō-ga arimasu.
B'yō-een-nee ee-koo hit-soo-yō-ga ah-ree-mahss.

How do you feel today?
Kyō-wa ikaga desu-ka?
K'yō-wa ee-ka-ga dess-ka?

Bad.
Warui.
Wa-roo-ee.

Better than yesterday.
Kinō yori ii desu.
Kee-nō yo-ree ee'ee dess.

Just fine!
Taihen ii desu!
Tai-hen ee'ee dess!

19. Dentist

In the unlikely event that the dentist should hurt you, tell him **Yamete, kudasai!** —"Stop, please!" or **Chotto matte, kudasai!**—"Wait a moment, please!" This will give you time to regain your courage.

Where is a good dentist?
Yoi haisha-wa doko desu-ka?
Yo-ee hai-sha-wa doh-ko dess-ka?

I have a toothache.
Ha-ga itai.
Ha-ga ee-tai.

This hurts.
Koko-ga itai.
Ko-ko-ga ee-tai.

Wait a minute!
Chotto matte!
Choht-toh maht-teh!

Stop, please!
Yamete, kudasai!
Ya-meh-teh, koo-da-sai!

You need a filling.
Ana-o tsumeru hitsuyō-ga arimasu.
Ah-na-o t'soo-meh-roo heet-soo-yō-ga ah-ree-mahss.

Will it take long?
Nagaku kakarimasu-ka?
Na-ga-koo ka-ka-ree-mahss-ka?

Fix it temporarily, please.
Kari-ni naoshite, kudasai.
Ka-ree-nee na-o-shee-teh, koo-da-sai.

We need to pull the tooth.
Kono ha-o nuku hitsuyō-ga arimasu.
Ko-no ha-o noo-koo heet-soo-yō-ga ah-ree-mahss.

An injection for pain, please.
Itami dome-no chūsha, dōzo.
Ee-ta-mee doh-meh-no chōō-sha, dōh-zo.

Now it's finished.
Ima dekimashita.
Ee-ma deh-kee-mahsh-ta.

Does it hurt?
Itai desu-ka?
Ee-tai dess-ka?

A little.
Sukoshi.
S'ko-shee.

Not at all!
Zen zen!
Zen zen!

Is that all?
Sore dake desu-ka?
So-reh da-keh dess-ka?

Yes, that's all!
Hai, sore dake!
Hai, so-reh da-keh!

What is the (honorable) charge?
O ikura desu-ka?
O ee-koo-ra dess-ka?

20. Problems and Police

Although the problems suggested below may never happen to you, the words are useful to know, just in case! Also, when addressing a policeman (**junsa**) don't forget to use the honorific, as in **junsa-san**.

Help!
Tasukete, kudasai!
Ta-soo-keh-teh, koo-da-sai!

Police!
Junsa-san!
Joon-sa-sahn!

What's wrong?
Dōshimashita-ka?
Dōh-shee-mahsh-ta-ka?

He stole my bag.
Watakushi-no kaban-o
  nusumimashita.
*Wa-tahk-shee-no ka-bahn-o
  noo-soo-mee-mahsh-ta.*

He took (my) wallet.
Kare-wa saifu-o torimashita.
Ka-reh-wa sai-foo-o toh-ree-mahsh-ta.

He stole (my) watch.
Tokei-o nusumimashita.
Toh-kei-o noo-soo-mee-mahsh-ta.

Catch that man!
Kare-o tsukamaete, kudasai!
Ka-reh-oh t'soo-ka-ma-eh-teh, koo-da-sai!

Wait!
Matte!
Maht-teh!

That's the man!
Sono hito desu!
So-no hee-toh dess!

I recognize him, officer.
Kare-o oboete imasu, junsa-san.
Ka-reh-o o-bo-eh-teh ee-mahss, joon-sa-sahn.

I am innocent!
Watakushi-wa muzai desu!
Wa-tahk-shee-wa moo-zai dess!

I didn't do anything!
Nani-mo shimasen deshita.
Na-nee-mo shee-ma-sen desh-ta!

I need a lawyer.
Bengoshi-ga hitsuyō desu.
Ben-go-shee-ga heet-soo-yō dess.

It's nothing.
Nan de mo nai desu.
Nahn deh mo nai dess.

It's a misunderstanding.
Gokai desu.
Go-kai dess.

Don't worry.
Shinpai nai.
Sheen-pai nai.

Can I go now?
Mō itte ii desu-ka?
Mō eet-teh ee'ee dess-ka?

I lost my traveler's checks.
Toraberāsu chekku-o nakushimashita.
To-ra-beh-ra-soo chek-koo-o na-koo-shee-mahsh-ta.

I lost my passport.
Pasupōto-o nakushimashita.
Pahs-pō-toh-o na-koo-shee-mahsh-ta.

Where is the American Embassy?
Amerika-no taishikan-wa doko desu-ka?
Ah-meh-ree-ka-no tai-shee-kahn-wa doh-ko dess-ka?

. . . the American Consulate?
Amerika-no ryōjikan . . .
Ah-meh-ree-ka-no r'yō-jee-kahn . . . ?

21. Traveling on Business

You will find the short phrases and vocabulary in this section extremely useful if you are on a business trip to Japan. Although English is the most prominent foreign language used in Japan and efficient interpreters are available, these phrases will add another dimension to your contacts with your Japanese business associates. The fact that you have taken the trouble to master some business expressions will be a compliment to your hosts and will indicate that you, by using their language, are reciprocating their traditional politeness.

Excuse me. Is this the office of the Tanaka Company?
Sumimasen. Tanaka Kaisha-no jimusho desu-ka?
Soo-mi-ma-sen. Ta-na-ka Kai-sha no jee-moo-sho dess-ka?

Is Mr. Tanaka in?
Tanaka-san imasu-ka?
Ta-na-ka-san ee-mahss-ka?

I have an appointment.
Yakusoku-ga arimasu.
Ya-koo-so-koo-ga ah-ree-mahss.

My name is Smith.
Watakushi-no namae-wa Sumisu desu.
Wa-ta-koo-shee-no na-ma-eh-wa Soo-mee-soo dess.

I am a representative of the Erikson Company.
Erikuson-no daihyō desu.
Eh-reek-sohn-no dai-h'yō dess.

. . . import and export.
. . . yunyū-to yushutsu.
. . . yoon-yōō-toh yoo-shoo-t'soo.

This is my card.
Kore-wa meishi desu.
Ko-reh-wa mey-shee dess.

One moment, please.
Chotto matte, kudasai.
Choht-toh maht-teh, koo-da-sai.

Hello, Mr. Tanaka?
Moshi, moshi. Tanaka-san?
Mo-shee, mo-shee. Ta-na-ka-san?

The Erikson Company representative is here.
Erikuson-Kaisha-no daihyō-ga koko-ni imasu.
Eh-reek-son-Kai-sha-no dai-h'yo-ga ko-ko-nee ee-mahss.

Are you Mr. Tanaka?
Tanaka-san desu-ka?
Ta-na-ka-sahn, dess-ka?

It is an honor (to meet you)!
Kōē-i desu!
Kō-ēy dess!

I received your letter.
O tegami-o uketorimashita.
O teh-ga-mee-o oo-keh-to-ree-mahsh-ta.

I am happy to be able to visit you.
Anata-o hōmon dekite ureshii desu.
Ah-na-ta-o hō-mohn deh-kee-teh oo-reh-shee'ee dess.

Welcome to Japan!
Nihon-ni yōkoso irrashaimashita!
Nee-hohn-nee yō-ko-so eer-ra-shai-mahsh-ta!

Thank you very much, Mr. Tanaka.
Dōmo arigatō gozaimasu, Tanaka-san.
Dōh-mo ah-ree-ga-tōh go-zai-mahss, Ta-na-ka-sahn.

We are interested in your products.
Anata-no seihin-ni kyōmi-ga arimasu.
Ah-na-ta-no sey-heen-nee k'yō-mee-ga ah-ree-mahss.

for example—radios, small TV sets,
tatoeba—rajio-to, chiisai terebi-to,
ta-toh-eh-ba—ra-jee-o-toh, chee'ee-sai teh-reh-bee-toh.

transistors, hi-fi equipment, and cameras.
toranjisutā-to, haifai kigu-to kamera.
toh-rahn-jee-sta-toh hai-fai kee-goo-toh ka-meh-ra.

Please give us copies of your catalog.
Dōzo katarogu-o kudasai.
Dōh-zo ka-ta-ro-goo-o koo-da-sai.

Certainly. Here are two copies.
Mochiron. Ni satsu dōzo.
Mo-chee-rohn. Nee saht-soo dōh-zo.

Is it possible to see your factory?
Kōjō-o miru kotoga dekimasu-ka?
Kō-jō-o mee-roo ko-toh-ga deh-kee-mahss-ka?

With pleasure.
Yorokonde.
Yo·ro-kohn-deh.

We will arrange a visit tomorrow.
Ashita hōmon suru tetsuzuki-o shimasu.
Ah-shee-ta hō-mohn soo-roo tet-soo-zoo-kee-o shee-mahss.

It was a pleasure to visit your factory.
Kōjō no hōmon-wa tanoshii deshita.
Kō-jō no hō-mohn-wa ta-no-shee'ee desh-ta.

The factory's operation is very efficient.
Kōjō-no keiei-ga taihen iki-todoite imasu.
Kō-jō-no kei-ei-ga tai-hen ee-kee-toh-doh-ee-teh ee-mahss.

We have studied your catalog.
Katarogu-o shirabemashita.
Ka-ta-ro-goo-o shee-ra-beh-mahsh-ta.

We wish to place an order.
Chūmon-o shitai desu.
Chō-mohn-o shee-tai dess.

We usually get 40 percent discount.
Tsūjyō yonjū-pāsento gurai-no waribiki-o moraimasu.
T'soō-j'yō yon-joō-pā-sen-toh gu-rai-no wa-ree-bee-kee-o mo-rai-mahss.

What are the terms of payment?
Shi harai jōken-wa nan desu-ka?
Shee ha-rai jō-ken-wa nahn dess-ka?

Ninety day bank draft.
Kyūjū nichi-no ginkō tegata.
K'yoō-joō nee-chee-no geen-kō teh-ga-ta.

Irrevocable letter of credit.
Ginkō-no shinyō-jō.
Geen-kō-no sheen-yō-jō.

Note: FOB and CIF are understood internationally.

When can we expect shipment to arrive?
Tsumini-wa itsu tsukimasu-ka?
T' soo-mee-nee-wa eet-soo t' soo-kee-mahss-ka?

Are these your best terms?
Saikō-no jōken desu-ka?
Sai-kō-no jō-ken dess-ka?

We wish to sign a contract.
Kei yaku-o shitai desu.
Keh-ee ya-koo-o shee-tai dess.

We are in agreement, aren't we?
Dōi shimasu-ne?
Dōy shee-mahss-neh?

We need time to examine the contract.
Keiyaku-sho-o shiraberu jikan-ga hitsuyō desu.
Keh-ee-ya-koo-sho-o shee-ra-beh-roo jee-kahn-ga hee-t' soo-yō dess.

Our lawyers will contact you.
Watakushi-domo-no bengoshi-kara renraku-o shimasu.
Wa-tahk-shee-doh-mo-no ben-go-shee-ka-ra ren-ra-koo-o shee-mahss.

We wish to invite you to dinner.
Watakushi-domo anata-o yūshoku-ni shōtai shitai desu.
Wa-tahk-shee-do-mo ah-na-ta-o yōō-sho-koo-nee shō-tai shee-tai dess.

We will come to your hotel at eight o'clock.
Anata-no hoteru-ni hachi-ji-ni kimasu.
Ah-na-ta-no ho-teh-roo-nee ha-chee-jee-nee kee-mahss.

Does your company manufacture automobiles?
Anata-no kaisha wa kuruma-no seizō-o shimasu-ka?
Ah-na-ta-no kai-sha wa koo-roo-ma-no sey-zō-o shee-mahss-ka?

Certainly. For cars (and) trucks (and) motorcycles
Mochiron. Jidōsha-to torakku-to mōtāsaikuru-to
Mo-chee-rohn. Jee-dōh-sha-toh toh-rahk-koo-toh mōh-tā-sai-koo-roo-toh

We have a factory in Kobe.
Kobe-ni kōjō-ga arimasu.
Ko-beh-nee kō-jō-ga ah-ree-mahss.

In addition, in America
Sore-to, Amerika-ni
So-reh-toh, Ah-meh-ree-ka-nee

we have an assembly plant.
kumitate kōjō-ga arimasu.
koo-mee-ta-teh kō-jō-ga ah-ree-mahss.

Does Japan import much from America?
Nihon-wa Amerika-kara takusan yunyū shimasu-ka?
Nee-hohn-wa Ah-meh-ree-ka-ka-ra ta-koo-sahn yoon-yōō shee-mahss-ka?

Yes, a lot.
Hai, takusan.
Hai, ta-koo-sahn.

We import meat (and) fruit (and) grain (and)
Niku-to, kudamon-to, kokumotsu-to
Nee-koo-toh, koo-da-mohn-to, ko-koo-mo-t'soo-toh

oil, and airplanes.
abura-to, hikōki-o yunyū shimasu.
ah-boo-ra-toh, hee-kō-kee-o yoon-yōō shee-mahss.

Also sports equipment.
Soreto supōtsu yōhin.
So-reh-toh soo-pō-t'soo yō-heen.

Thank you for a very nice time.
Tanoshii jikan-o arigatō gozaimashita.
Ta-no-shee'ee jee-kahn-o ah-ree-ga-tōh go-zai-mahsh-ta.

Thank you for everything!
Iro iro arigatō gozaimashita!
Ee-ro ee-ro ah-ree-ga-tōh go-zai-mahsh-ta!

It was a pleasure to meet you.
Ome-ni kakarete ureshii deshita.
O-meh-nee ka-ka-reh-teh oo-reh-shee'ee desh-ta.

It is a pleasure doing business with you.
Anata-to shigoto-ga dekite ureshii desu.
Ah-na-ta-toh shee-go-toh-ga deh-kee-teh oo-reh-shee'ee dess.

When you visit America,
Amerika-ni hōmon-o shimasu toki,
Ah-meh-ree-ka-nee hō-mohn-o shee-mahss to-kee,

please be sure to come see us.
zehi tazunete kudasai.
zeh-hee ta-zoo-neh-teh koo-da-sai.

22. A New Type of Dictionary

The following dictionary supplies a list of English words and their translations into Japanese, which will enable you to make up your own sentences in addition to those given in the phrase book. By using these words, in conjunction with the following advice and shortcuts, you will be able to make up hundreds of sentences by yourself. In general, only one Japanese equivalent is given for each English word—the one most useful to you—so you will not be in doubt about which word to use.

We have not given the pronunciation in the dictionary, because it conforms with the easy pronunciation of the Japanese words already given in the sections you have read so far. Remember that a line over a vowel prolongs the pronunciation of that vowel.

By using this dictionary, it is relatively easy to learn to speak simple Japanese. Ordinary day-to-day conversation in Japanese has certain advantages over other foreign languages.

One advantage of Japanese grammar is that it has a series of special syllables which identify and indicate the function of the word to which they are attached; they indicate what is happening, who or what is doing the action, and help to clarify the meaning of a sentence. They and their function are as follows:

-wa (or) **-ga** indicates the subject

-o indicates the object
-ni indicates the indirect object and also means *at, for, to*
-no indicates the possessive
-e indicates *to* (direction)
-kara indicates *from*
-made indicates *up to, toward*
-de indicates *at* (or) *in* (where an action occurs)
-to indicates *with* (or) *and*, used in a series
-ka is a spoken question mark that comes at the end of a sentence
-ne added to a verb indicates *isn't it?, isn't it so?, don't you think so?, well* . . . (In the latter case it serves as a conversational bridge or stopgap.)

In the preceding chapters we have connected these syllables to the words they affect by a hyphen to show that they are not part of the word but are separate, according to the meaning desired, as in the following:

hotel = **hoteru**   he = **kare**
hotel (subject) = **hoteru-wa**   he (subject) = **kare-wa**
hotel (object) = **hoteru-o**   him = **kare-o**
(of the) hotel = **hoteru-no**   his = **kare-no**
(to, at, for) the hotel = **hoteru-ni** (to, for) him = **kare-ni**
(from) the hotel = **hoteru-kara**   (from) him = **kare-kara**

Occasionally **-ni** follows an adjective, making it an adverb:
shizuka = quiet   **shizuka-ni** = quietly

A (**na**) or (**no**) written after an adjective means that **na** or **no** must follow *if* the adjective comes before the noun.

She is beautiful. = **Kirei desu.**
She is a beautiful woman. = **Kirei na onna desu.**

Observe the three indicators used in the following sentence:

I see your car. = **Watakushi-wa anata-no kurama-o mimasu.**

Here you have **-wa** for the subject, **-no** for the possessive, and **-o** for the direct object, the order of the words being: I your car see. By changing the arrangements of the suffix syllables and adding a **-ka** for a question you have:

Anata-wa watakushi-no kuruma-o mimasu-ka? = You my car (do you) see?

If you remember to use the suffixes and always place the verb at the end of the sentence, you will find it is easy, effective, and enjoyable to form your own sentences in Japanese.

The verb does not change its action according to who is doing the action; that is, there is only one form for each tense. The present form of **desu** (to be) can mean "am," "is," or "are." There is a basic form for every verb ending in **u** and also a more polite form ending in **-masu.** In the dictionary this polite form is indicated in parentheses *after* the basic form of each verb. If you look up "to go", you will find **iku** followed by (**ikimasu**). Both versions are in the present tense, but it is better and easier for you to use the polite form within the parentheses. The present form can also mean the future (I will go) if you add "tomorrow," "next week," or some other word suggesting the future. The negative is made by changing **-masu** to **-masen.** The past tense can be formed by changing **-masu** to **-mashita,** and the past negative by changing **-mashita** to **masen deshita.** A probable future, also equivalent to "probably" or "let's" can be formed by changing the polite verb ending to **mashō.**

Observe how this works with a typical verb "to go" always using the polite form of the verbs. It applies to all forms: I, you, he, she, we, etc.

ikimasu = go, will go
ikimasen = do not go, won't go
ikimashita = went
ikimasen deshita = didn't go
ikimashō = let's go

The most polite way of making a request is to use **kudasai:**

"The check, please." = **Okanjō-o kudasai.**

To use a verb with **kudasai**, shorten the polite form and add **-te** or, sometimes, **-de.**

Kuru (kimasu) means "to come," so take the **-masu** from the polite form and substitute **-te:** "Please come." = **Kite kudasai.**

Although **kudasai** implies "please", there is another word— **dōzo**—often used with it. (In Japanese one can never be too polite!)

For a command in the negative take the basic verb, the one ending in **-u**, and add **hitsuyō-wa arimasen:** "Please don't come." = **Kuru hitsuyō-wa arimasen.** With customary politeness you are really saying "To come there is no need."

This basic verb form is often the one to use in combinations with other verbs to express concepts such as "must," "ought," "wish," "can," "want," "when," "to be able," "unable," the conditional with "if," and others.

All of these special constructions are explained in short notes within the following dictionary. At the end of the dictionary you will find a "Point to the Answer" section written in Japanese and English, which you will find especially useful if you have occasion to travel outside the cities around the beautiful Japanese countryside.

A _____

(to be) able	dekimasu
about	oyoso
above	ue-ni
absent	fuzai
accident	jiko
account (bank)	kōza
account (bill)	o-kanjō
across	mukōgawa-ni
actor (or) **actress**	haiyū
address	jūsho
(to) admire	kanshin suru (kanshin shimasu)
advertisement	kōkoku
advice	chūkoku
(to be) afraid	kowagaru (kowagarimasu)
Africa	Afurika
after	ato-ni, ato-de
afternoon	gogo
again	mata
age	toshi
agent	dairisha
ago	mae-ni
(to) agree	dōisuru (dōishimasu)
air	kūki
airplane	hikōki
airport	kūkō
all	subete-no, subete
That's all!	Mō kore dake!
(to) allow	yurusu (yurushimasu)
all right	yoroshii
almost	hotondo
alone	hitori-de
already	sude-ni
also	mo, mata

always	itsu de mo
am	imasu (or) desu
America	Amerika
American (person)	Amerika-jin
amusing	omoshiroi, tanoshii
ancient	mukashi
and	-to (for objects), soshite (for phrases)
(to be) angry	okotte iru (okotte imasu)
animal	dōbutsu
annoying	mendō (na)
another	hoka
answer	henji
antiseptic	bōfuzai
anyone, anybody	dare de mo
anything	nan de mo
anywhere	doko de mo
anyway	tonikaku
apartment	apārto
apple	ringo
appointment	yakusoku
Arab (person)	Arabia-jin
architect	kenchikuka
architecture	kenchiku-yōshiki
are	desu, imasu (or) arimasu
(there) are	arimasu
arm	ude
army	rikugun
around	mawari-ni
(to) arrive	tōchaku suru (tōchaku shimasu)
art	geijutsu
artist	geijutsuka
as	no-yō-ni
Asia	Ajia
(to) ask	tazuneru (tazunemasu)

aspirin	asupirin
at	-ni, -de
(the) Atlantic	Taiseiyō
atom	genshi
aunt (yours)	oba-san
aunt (mine)	oba
Australia	Ōsutorariya
Australian (person)	Ōsutorariya-jin
author	sakka
automatic	jidō (no)
automobile	jidōsha
autumn	aki
average	heikin

B

baby	akanbō
back (body)	senaka
bad	warui
badly	waruku
baggage	nimotsu
bank	ginkō
banker	ginkōka
bath	ofuro
battery	denchi
battle	tatakai
(to) be	desu, imasu (for persons or living things), arimasu (for inanimate things)
beach	hamabe
beans	mame
beautiful	utsukushii

because	naze-naraba
bed	shindai
bedroom	shinshitsu
beef	gyūniku
before	mae ni
(to) begin	hajimaru (hajimarimasu)
behind	ushiro-ni
(to) believe	shinjiru (shinjimasu)
belt	bando
beside	no soba-ni
best	saikō (no)
better	motto yoi
between	aida
big	ōkii
bill (account)	o-kanjō
bird	tori
birthday	tanjōbi
black	kuroi
blanket	mōfu
blond	kinpatsu
blood	chi
blue	aoi
boat	fune
book	hon
bookstore	honya
born (was or were)	umare-mashita
both	r'yōhō
bottle	bin
bottom	soko
box	hako
boy	danshi
brain	zunō
brake (car)	burēki
bread	pan
(to) break	kowasu (kowashimasu)

breakfast	asahan
breast	mune
breath	iki
bridge	hashi
briefcase	kaban
(to) bring	motte kuru (motte kimasu)
Bring, please	. . . motte kite, kudasai.
broken	kowareta
(my) elder brother	ani
(my) younger brother	otōto
(your) elder brother	onīi-san
(your) younger brother	otōto-san
brown	cha iro
brush (for writing)	fude
brush (for hair)	atama-no burashi
brush (for teeth)	ha-burashi
(a) Buddhist	bukkyō-to
building	tatemono
bus	basu
business (big)	jitsugyō
business (small)	shōbai
busy	isogashii
but	shikashi
butter	batā
button	botan
(to) buy	kau (kaimasu)
by	no soba ni

C

cake	kēki
(to) call	yobu (yobimasu)

(to) call (telephone)	kakeru (kakemasu)
camera	kamera
can (to be able)	dekiru (dekimasu)
cannot	dekimasen

When a second verb is employed, use its infinitive form followed by *koto-ga* and *dekimasu*:

Can you come?	*Kuru koto-ga dekimasu-ka?*
I can't come.	*Kuru koto-ga dekimasen.*

can (container)	kan
can opener	kankiri
Canada	Kanada
Canadian (person)	Kanada-jin
candy	kyandē
capital (city)	shuto
captain (ship)	senchō
car (automobile)	jidōsha
card (business)	meishi
carefully	ki-o tsukete
carrot	ninjin
(to) carry	hakobu (hakobimasu)
cash	genkin
cashier	kaikei-kakari
castle	o shiro
cat	neko
center	chūshin
certificate	shōmeisho
chair	isu
(to) change	kaeru (kaemasu)
cheap	yasui
check (bank)	kogitte
cheese	chīīzu

cherry (fruit)	sakuranbō
cherry blossom	sakura
chest (body)	mune
chest (box)	hako
chicken	tori
child	kodomo
China	Chūgoku
Chinese (language)	Chūgoku-go
Chinese (person)	Chūgoku-jin
chocolate	chokolēto
church	kyōkai
chopsticks	o-hashi
cigarette	shigaretto (or) tabako
citizen	shimin
city	shi
clean	seiketsu-(na)
cleaner's	sōjiki
clever	rikō na
climate	kikō
close (near)	chikai
(to) close	shimeru (shimemasu)
closed	shimatta
clothing (Japanese)	kimono
clothing (western)	yōfuku
cloud	kumo
coffee	kōhī
coffee shop	kōhī shoppu
cold	samui
cold (illness)	hana kaze
college	daigaku
color	iro
comb	kushi
(to) come	kuru (kimasu)
(to) come back	kaeru (kaerimasu)
Come in!	Ohairinasai!

comfortable	raku na
communist (person)	kyōsan shugisha
company	kaisha
competition	kyōsō-aite
computer	konpyūtā
Congratulations!	Omedetō!
conservative (person)	hoshuteki (na)
consulate	ryōjikan
(to) continue	tsuzukeru (tsuzukemasu)
conversation	kaiwa
cook (chef)	kokku-san
(to) cook	ryori suru (ryōri shimasu)
cookies	okashi
(a) copy	utsushi
corner	kado
correct	tadashii
(the) cost	nedan
cotton	wata
cough	seki
country	kuni
cow	meushi
crab	kani
(to) cry	naku (nakimasu)
cup	koppu
customer	kyaku
customs (office)	zeikan
(to) cut	kiru (kirimasu)

D

(to) dance	odoru (odorimasu)
dangerous	abunai

dark	kurai
date (appointment)	yakusoku
date (calendar)	hi nichi
daughter	musume
(your daughter)	ojōsan
day	nichi
dear (affection)	shinai (na)
December	jūnigatsu
deck (boat)	kanpan
deep	fukai
deer	shika
delayed	okureta
delicious	oishii
(to) deliver	todokeru (todokemasu)
dentist	haisha
department store	depāto
dessert	dezāto
devil	akuma
dictionary	jibiki

did: To express did, change the *-masu* of the polite form to *-mashita*. **Did you hear?** *Kikimashita-ka?*

did not: Change the *-mashita* to *-masen deshita*. **I did not hear.** *Kikimasen deshita.*

different	chigai
difficult	muzukashii
dining room	shokudō
dinner	yūhan
direction	hōkō
director	torishimari-yaku
disappointment	shitsubō
discount	waribiki
distance	kyori

do (for questions): add *-ka* to the *masu* of the verb:

I understand.—*Wakarimasu*.

Do you understand? *Wakarimasu-ka?*

do not (or) **don't**: Modify the *masu* of the verbal construction to *masen*.

I see.—*Mimasu*.

I don't see.—*Mimasen*.

Don't! To urge someone politely *not* to do something, you say the action isn't *necessary*. Use the infinitive form of the verb followed by *hitsuyō wa nai*.

Don't leave!—*Deru hitsuyō wa nai!*

dock	hatoba
doctor	isha
dog	inu
doll	ningyō
dollar	doru
door	to
down	shita
dress	doresu
(to) drink	nomu (nomimasu)
(to) drive	unten suru (unten shimasu)
driver	untenshu
drugstore	yakkyoku
(to be) drunk	yotte imasu
duck	kamo

E

each	meimei
ear	mimi
early	hayai

earthquake	jishin
east	higashi
easy	yasashii
(to) eat	taberu (tabemasu)
eggs	tamago
eight	hachi
eighteen	jūhachi
eighty	hachijū
either	dochira de mo
electric	denki
elephant	zō
elevator	erebētā
eleven	jūichi
embassy	taishikan
emerald	emerarudo
emergency	kinkyū
emperor	tennō
employee	shiyōnin
empty	kara
end	owari
England	Eikoku
English (the language)	Ei-go
English (a person)	Eikoku-jin
enough	jūbun
(to) enter	hairu (hairimasu)
entertaining	omoshiroi, yukai-na
entrance	iriguchi
envelope	fūtō
equipment	setsubi
error	machigai
especially	toku-ni
estimate	mitsumori
Europe	Yōroppa
European (a person)	Yōroppa-jin
even (adv.)	de mo

evening	yūgata
ever	itsuka
every (each)	ono-ono
everybody	mina-san
everything	nan de mo
everywhere	doko de mo
exactly	seikaku-ni
(to) examine	kensa suru (kensa shimasu)
excellent	yūshū (na)
except	no hoka ni
(to) exchange	kōkan suru (kōkan shimasu)
Excuse me!	Gomen nasai! (or) sumimasen
exercise	renshū
exhibition	tenjikai
exit	deguchi
(to) expect	kitai suru (kitai shimasu)
expenses	hiyō
expensive	takai
explanation	setsumei
(to) export	yushutsu suru (yushutsu shimasu)
express mail	sokutatsu
express train	kyūkō-ressha
extra	yobun no
eye	me

F

face	kao
factory	kōba (or) kōjyō
fall (autumn)	aki
(to) fall	ochiru (ochimasu)

family	kazoku
(your) family	go-kazoku
famous	yūnei
fan	uchiwa
far	tōi
How far?	Dono gurai tōi desu-ka?
fare	ryōkin
farm	nōjō
farther	motto tōi
fast	hayaku
fat	futotta
(my) father	chichi
(your) father	otō-san
fault	kashitsu
February	Nigatsu
feeling	kibun
fence	kakine
fever	netsu
few	sukoshi
fiancé or fiancée (both sexes)	iinazuki
field (land)	hatake
fifteen	jūgo
fifty	gojū
(to) fight	tatakau (tatakaimasu)
film	fuirumu
final	saishū-no
(to) find	mitsukeru (mitsukemasu)
fine (health)	genki
Fine!	Ii!
fine (penalty)	bakkin
finger	yubi
(to) finish	owaru (owarimasu)
fire	hi
first	ichiban
fish	sakana

fishing	tsuri
five	go (or) itsutsu
(to) fix	naosu (naoshimasu)
flag	hata
flight	hikō
floor	yuka
floor (of building)	kai
flower	hana
fly (insect)	hai
(to) fly	tobu (tobimasu)
food	tabemono
foot	ashi
for	-no-tame-ni
forbidden	kinjita
foreigner	gaikokujin
forest	hayashi
(to) forget	wasureru (wasuremasu)
Don't forget!	Wasure nai!
fork	fōku
forty	yonjū
four	shi, yon (or) yottsu
fourteen	jūshi
fox	kitsune
France	Furansu
free	tada
freight	kamotsu
French (language)	Furansu-go
French (person)	Furansu-jin
frequently	shiba shiba
fresh	shinsen (na)
Friday	Kinyōbi
fried	furaido
friend	tomodachi
from	kara
(in) front of	mae-ni

fruit	kudamono
full	ippai
funny	okashii
fur	kegawa
furniture	kagu
future	shōrai

G

game	asobi
game (sports)	kyōgi
garage	garēji
garden	niwa
gasoline	gasorin
gas station	gasorin stando
generally	tsūjyō
gentleman	shimshi
German (language)	Doitsu-go
German (a person)	Doitsu-jin
Germany	Doitsu
(to) get (receive)	morau (moraimasu)
(to) get off	oriru (orimasu)
(to) get up	okiru (okimasu)
gift	okurimono
girl	musume (or) onna-no-ko
(to) give (to other person)	ageru (agemasu)
(to) give (other person gives to you)	kureru (kudasaimasu)

Japanese politeness implies that, in giving to another person, you are raising the gift to his higher level (*ageru*), but when someone gives you something, he passes it down to your lower level (*kudaisaimasu*).

Give me, please. *Watakushi-ni kudasai.*

gladly	yorokonde
glass (for windows)	garasu
glass (drinking)	koppu
glasses	megane
glove	tebukuro
(to) go	iku (ikimasu)
Let's go!	ikimashō!
(to) go in	hairu (hairimasu)
(to) go out	deru (demasu)
God	Kami-sama
gold	kin
golf	gorufu
good	ii (or) yoi
Good afternoon!	Konnichi-wa!
good-bye	sayōnara
Good morning!	Ohayō!
Good evening!	Konban-wa!
government	seifu
gradually	dan dan
(a) graduate	sotsugyo sei
granddaughter	mago musume
grandfather	ojīi-san
grandmother	obā-san
grandson	mago-musuko
grapefruit	gurēpu furūtsu
grapes	budō
gray	nezumi iro
great	idai (na)
green	midori iro
ground	jimen

(to) grow	sodatsu (sodachimasu)
guarantee	hoshō
guest	okyaku
guide (person)	annaisha, gaido
gun	teppō

H _____

hair	kami no ke
half	hanbun
ham	hamu
hand	te
handbag	hando-bakku
happy	ureshii
harbor	minato
hard (difficult)	muzukashii
hat	bōshi
(to) have	motte iru (motte imasu) (or) arimasu

To express **"Have you?"** informally, use —*ga arimasu-ka?*
Have you a match? *Macchi-ga arimasu-ka?* **have to** Use
the basic verb followed by—*nakereba narimasen.*

he	kare (or) anohito
head	atama
headacne	zutsū
healthy	kenkō (na)
(to) hear	kiku (kikimasu)
heart	shinzō

heavy	omoi
Hello! (on phone)	Moshi moshi!
(to) help	tasukeru (tasukemasu)
Help!	Tasukete!
her (object)	kanojo-o
her (possessive)	kanojo-no
(to) her	kanojo-ni
here	koko
high	takai
hill	oka
him	kare-o
(to) him	kare-ni
his	kare-no
history	rekishi
hole	ana
holiday	saijitsu
home	uchi
honey	hachimitsu
(to) hope	nozomu (nozomimasu)
horse	uma
hospital	byōin
hot	atsui
hotel	hoteru
hotel (Japanese style)	ryokan
hour	jikan
house	uchi
how	dō
How far?	Dono kurai arimasu-ka?
How long?	Dono kurai desu-ka?
How many?	Ikutsu gurai desu-ka?
How much?	Ikura desu-ka?
however	shikashi nagara
hundred	hyaku
hungry (wishing to eat)	tabetai
hunting	kari

(to) hurry	isogu (isogimasu)
Hurry!	Hayaku!
husband	otto
(my) husband	shujin
(your) husband	go-shujin

I

I	watakushi
ice	kōri
ice cream	aisukurīmu
Idiot!	Baka!
if	moshi (A supposition following "if" is expressed by substituting *-mashitara* for the *-masu* ending of the verb. If he comes. *Moshi kimashitara*.)
ill	byōki
imitation	mane
immediately	sugi (ni)
(to) import	yunyū suru (yunyū shimasu)
important	jūyō
importer	yunyū gyōsha
impossible	fukanō
in, inside of	-no naka-ni
(to) include	fukumu (fukumimasu)
income	shotoku (or) shūnyū
inconvenience	fuben
India	Indo
Indian (a person)	Indo-jin
indigestion	fushōka
Indonesia	Indonesiya

Indonesian (a person)	Indonesiya-jin
industry	sangyō
inhabitant	jūmin
information	annai
inn (Japanese style)	ryokan
(to) inquire	tazuneru (tazunemasu)
inquiry	chōsa
insect	mushi
instead of	-no kawari-ni
intelligent	rikō (na)
interesting	omoshiroi
international	kokusai-teki (na)
interpreter	tsūyaku
interview	menkai
(to) introduce	shōkai suru (shōkai shimasu)
(to) invite	shōtai suru (shōtai shimasu)
iron (metal)	tetsu
island	shima
Isn't that so?	So desu-ne?
Israel	Isuraeru
Israeli (a person)	Isuraeru-jin
Ireland	Airurando
Irish (a person)	Airurando-jin
it	use "this," *kore* or "that," *sore*.
Italian (the language)	Itarī-go
Italian (a person)	Itarī-jin
Italy	Itarī
ivory	zōge

J

jade	hisui

January	Ichigatsu
Japan	Nihon
Japanese (the language)	Nihon-go
Japanese (a person)	Nihon-jin
Jew	Yudaya-jin
jewelry	hōseki
job	shigoto
joke	jōdan
July	Shichigatsu
June	Rokugatsu
just (exactly)	chōdo
Just now.	Tada ima.

K

key	kagi
(to) kill	korosu (koroshimasu)
kilometer	kiromētā
kind (sort)	shurui
kind (good hearted)	shinsetsu (na)
king	ōsama
kiss	kisu
kitchen	daidokoro
knee	hiza
knife	hōchō, naifu
(to) know	shiru (shirimasu)
Do you know . . . ?	Shirimasu-ka?
I don't know.	Shirimasen.
Korea	Kankoku
Korean (the language)	Kankoku-go
Korean (a person)	Kankoku-jin

L

ladies' room	onna-no otearai
lady	fujin
lake	mizu-umi
lamp	ranpu
land	riku
language	gengo
large	ōkii
last	saigo no
late	osoi
later	ato de
(to) laugh	warau (waraimasu)
lavatory	tearaijo
lawyer	bengoshi
(to) learn	narau (naraimasu)
leather	kawa
(to) leave	saru (sarimasu)
left	hidari
leg	ashi
lemon	remon
let's	Use-*mashō* instead of -*masu* as the verb ending.
Let's go!	Ikimashō!
letter	tegami
license	menkyo
light (electric)	denki
(to) like	suki desu
Do you like _____?	_____-ga suki desu-ka?
like this (in this way)	kono yō-ni
linen	rinneru
lion	shishi
lipstick	kuchibeni
list	hyō
(to) listen	kiku (kikimasu)

little	chiisai
a little	sukoshi
just a little	sukoshi dake
(to) live	sumu (sumimasu)
Where are you living?	Doko ni sunde imasu-ka?
lobster	ise ebe
long	nagai
(to) look	miru (mimasu)
Look out!	Chūi!
(to) lose	nakusu (nakushimasu)
lost	nakushimashita
(to) love	aisu (aishimasu)
I love you!	Watakushi-wa anata-o aishimasu!
low	hikui
Good luck!	Gokōun-o inorimasu!
luggage	nimotzu
lunch	hirugohan

M

machine	kikai
madame	okusan
made	tsukutta
made in Japan.	Nihon sei.
maid	meido-san
mail	yūbin
(to) make	tsukuru (tsukurimasu)
magazine	zasshi
Malaya	Marei
man	otoko
manager	shihainin

(to) manufacture	sēzōsuru (sēzōshimasu)
many	takusan (no)
map	chizu
March	Sangatsu
market	ichiba
married	kekkonshita
marvelous	subarashii
massage	massāji
match	macchi
May	Gogatsu
maybe	tabun
me	watakushi-o
(to) or **(for) me**	watakushi-ni
(from) me	watakushi-kara
(with) me	watakushi-to
meat	niku
mechanic	shokunin
medicine	kusuri
(to) meet	au (aimasu)
Happy to meet you!	Hajimemashite!
member	kaiin
mens' room	otoko-no otearai
message	messēji
meter	mētoru
middle	chūkan
might	(see **could**)
milk	miruku
million	hyakuman
mind	kokoro
minute	fun
mirror	kagami
mistake	machigai
misunderstanding	gokai
model	moderu
modern	modan

One moment!	Chotto!
Monday	Getsyōbi!
money	okane
monk	sōryō
monkey	saru
month	gatsu (or) getsu
moon	tsuki
more	motto
more____than____	motto____yori____
morning	asa
mosquito	ka
most	ichiban (literally "number one")
(my) mother	haha
(your) mother	okā-san
motor	mōtā
motorcycle	mōtāsaikuru
mountain	yama
mouse	nezumi
mouth	kuchi
(to) move (something)	ugokasu (ugokashimasu)
movie	eiga
Mr. Mrs. Miss	Add "san" to name.
much	takusan (no)
museum	hakubutsukan
music	ongaku
musician	ongakuka
must	Use basic verb, adding *nakereba narimasen*.
mustache	hige
my (or) mine	watakushi (no)
mind	zunō

N

name	namae
narrow	semai
nation	kokka
nature	shizen
natural	shizen-no
navy	kaigun
near	chikai
necessary	hitsuyō
neck	kubi
necktie	nekutai
(to) need	iru (irimasu) (or) hitsuyō desu
nephew	oi
nervous	shinkei (no)
Netherlands	Oranda
never	zen zen
Never mind!	Kamaimasen!
nevertheless	sore de mo
new	atarashii
news	nyū-su
newspaper	shinbun
New Year	shinnen
next	tsugi (no)
niece	mei
night	yoru
nightclubs	naito kurabu
nine	ku, kyu (or) kokonotsu
nineteen	jūku
ninety	kyūjū
no	iie
nobody	daremo (followed by verb in negative)
noisy	sōzōshii

none	nanimo (followed by verb in negative)
north	kita
North America	Kita Amerika
nose	hana
not	nai
not yet	mada
nothing	nanimo (followed by verb in negative)
November	Jūichigatsu
now	ima
nowhere	doko ni mo (followed by verb in negative)
number	ban (or) bango

O

(to) obtain	morau (moraimasu)
occasionally	toki doki
occupation	shokugyō
ocean	kaiyō
o'clock	-ji
October	Jūgatsu
(to) offer	teikyō suru (teikyō shimasen)
office	jimusho
officer (military)	shikan
officer (of corporation)	yakuin
often	shiba shiba
oil	abura
(it's) okay	ii desu
old (for people)	toshiyori
old (for things)	furui

omelet	omuretsu
on	-no ue-ni
once	ichido
Once more!	Mō ichido!
At once!	Sugu-ni!
one	ichi (or) hitotsu
onion	tamanegi
only	dake
(to) open	akeru (akemasu)
opinion	iken
opportunity	kikai
or	mata wa
orange	orenji
order (commercial)	chūmon
orient	tōyō
oriental	tōyō no
other	hoka no
ought to	beki desu (used after infinitive form of verb to which "ought" refers)
our, ours	watakushidomo-no
outside	-soto-ni
over	ue-ni
overcoat	gaitō
over there	asoko-ni
(to) owe	karite iru (karite imasu)
owner	mochinushi
oyster	kaki

P

Pacific Ocean	Tai Heiyō
package	kozutsumi

paid	haraimashita
painful	itai
palace	kyūden
paper	kami
Pardon me!	Gomen nasai!
parents	ryōshin
park	kōen
(to) park	chūsha suru (chūsha shimasu)
part (machine)	buhin
partner	nakama
party	kai
passenger	jōkyaku
passport	ryoken
patent	tokkyo
(to) pay	shiharau (shiharimasu)
payment	shiharai
payment in cash	genkin de shiharai
payment by check	kogitte de shiharai
peace	heiwa
peach	momo
pear	nasi
pearl	shinju
pen	mannenhitsu
pencil	enpitsu
people	hitobito
percentage	buai
perfect	kanzenna
perfume	kōsui
perhaps	tabun
person	hito
Philippines	Firippin
Filipino (person)	Firippin-jin
photo	shashin
picture	e
(one) piece	ikko

pier	sanbashi
pill	ganyaku
pillow	makura
pin	pin
pink	momo iro
place	tokoro
plastic	purasuchikku
plate	sara
(to) play	asobu (asobimasu)
pleasant	tanoshii
please	dōzo
pocket	poketto
pocketbook	techō
poem	shi
poison	doku
police	keisatsu
policeman	junsa, keikan
polite	teinei (na)
poor	binbō (na)
port	minato
Portugal	Porutogaru
Portuguese (language)	Porutogaru-go
Portuguese (person)	Porutogaru-jin
(to be) possible	dekiru (dekimasu)
postage stamp	kitte
postcard	hagaki
(to) prefer	konomu (konomimasu)
preparation	shitaku
present (gift)	okurimono
president (of company)	shachō
president (of country)	daitōryō
pretty	kawaii
price	nedan
priest	shinpu
print (woodcut)	hanga

private	shiyō-no
problem	mondai
(to) produce	seisan suru (seisan shimasu)
production	seisan
profession	shokugyō
profits	rieki
program	puroguramu
(to) promise	yakusoku (yakusoku shimasu)
proposal	teian
public	ōyake no
publicity	senden
(to) publish	shuppan suru (shuppan shimasu)
(to) pull	hiku (hikimasu)
pure	junsui
purple	murasaki
(to) push	osu (oshimasu)
(to) put	oku (okimasu)

Q

quality	hinshitsu
quantity	bunryō
question	shitsumon
quick	hayai
quickly	hayaku
quiet	shizuka (na)
quite	mattaku
quilt	futon

R

rabbit	usagi
race (contest)	kyōsō
race (ethnic)	jinshu
radio	rajio
railroad	tetsudō
rain	ame
raincoat	reinkōto
rapidly	sumiyaka-ni
rat	nezumi
rate	sōba
rather	mushiro
raw	nama-no
raw material	genryō
razor	kamisori
(to) read	yomu (yomimasu)
ready	dekimashita
Is it ready?	Dekimashita-ka?
real	shinjitsu-no
really	honto-ni
reason	riyū
receipt	ryōshūsho
(to) receive	uketoru (uketorimasu)
recently	kono aida
(to) recognize	mitomeru (mitomemasu)
(to) recommend	suisen suru (suisen shimasn)
red	akai
refrigerator	reizōko
My regards to _____	(the name, then) . . . -ni yoroshiku
regular	teiki-teiki (na)
religion	shūkyō
(to) remain	todo maru (todo marimasu)
(to) remember	omoidasu (omoidashimasu)

(to) rent	kariru (karimasu)
(to) repair	shūri suru (shūri shimasu)
(to) represent	daihyō suru (daihyō shimasu)
representative	daihyōsha
responsible	sekinin
(to) rest	yasumu (yasumimasu)
restaurant (Japanese style)	ryōriya
restaurant (Western style)	resutoran
(to) return	kaeru (kaerimasu)
revolution	kakumei
rice (cooked)	gohan
rice (uncooked)	kome
rich	kanemochi (na)
(to) ride	noru (norimasu)
right (direction)	migi
To the right!	Migi e!
right (not wrong)	tadashii
Right away!	Sugu-ni!
ring	yubiwa
river	kawa
road	michi
robber	gōtō
Roman letter	Rōmaji
roof	yane
room	heya
round	marui
round (trip)	ōfuku
ruby	rubī
(to) run	hashiru (hashirimasu)
Russia	Roshiya
Russian (language)	Roshiya-go
Russian (person)	Roshiya-jin

S _____

sad	kanashii
safe (not dangerous)	anzen
safe	kinko
sailor	suihei
salad	sarada
salary	kyūryō
sales manager	shihainin
salesman (representative)	sērusuman
salesperson (store)	uriko
salmon	shake
same	onaji
sandals	zōri (or) geta
sandwich	sandoicchi
Saturday	Doyōbi
(to) say	yū (iimasu)
school	gakkō
science	kagaku
scientist	kagakusha
scissors	hasami
screen	byōbu
sea	umi
seat	seki
secretary	hisho
(to) see	miru (mimasu)
(to) sell	uru (urimasu)
(to) separate	wakeru (wakemasu)
September	Kugatsu
service	sābisu
seven	shichi (or) nanatsu
seventeen	jūshichi
seventy	shichijū
several	ikutsuka-no
shall	(see **will**)

shampoo	shanpū
shark	same
she	kanojo
sheep	hitsuji
ship	fune
shipment	funa-zumi
shirt	shatsu
shoe	kutsu
shop	mise
short	mijikai
should (obligation)	Use infinitive of verb followed by *beki desu.*
shoulder	kata
(to) show	miseru (misemasu)
Please show me!	Misete kudasai!
shower (rain)	yūdachi
shower (bath)	shawā
shrimps	chiisai ebi
shrine	jinja
(to) shut	shimeru (shimemasu)
sick	byōki
sightseeing	kankō
silk	kinu
silver	gin
(to) sing	utau (utaimasu)
sister	shimai
(my) elder sister	ane
(my) younger sister	imōto
(your) elder sister	onēsan
(your) younger sister	imōtosan
(to) sit (on floor)	suwaru (suwarimasu)
(to) sit (on chair)	koshikakeru (koshikakemasu)
six	roku
sixteen	jūroku
sixty	rokujū

size	sunpō
skirt	sukāto
sky	sora
(to) sleep	nemuru (nemurimasu)
slowly	yukkuri
small	chiisai
smell	nioi
(to) smoke	tabako-o suu (tabako-o suimasu)
snake	hebi
snow	yuki
so	so
soap	sekken
sock	kutsu shita
soft	yawaraka (na)
sold	ureta
soldier	heitai
somebody	dareka
something	nanika
sometimes	toki doki
somewhere	dokoka
(my) son	musuko
(your) son	musuko-san
song	uta
soon	mamonaku
(I'm) sorry!	Gomen nasai!
soup	sūpu
south	minami
South America	Minami Amerika
South American	Minami Amerika-jin
Spain	Supein
Spanish (language)	Supein-go
Spanish (person)	Supein-jin
(to) speak	hanasu (hanashimasu)
(to) spend	tsukau (tsukaimasu)
splendid	rippa (na)
spoon	saji

sport	supōtsu
spring (season)	haru
stamp	kitte
(to) stand	tatsu (tachimasu)
star	hoshi
station (railroad)	eki
statue	zō
steel	hagane
still	mada
stock market	kabushiki-torihikijō
stocks	kabuken
stone	ishi
(to) stop	tomaru (tomarimasu)
Stop!	Tomarinasai!
store	mise
storm	arashi
straight (ahead)	massugu-ni
strange	mezurashii
street	michi
strong	tsuyoi
student	gakusei
(to) study	benkyō suru (benkyō shimasu)
style	sutairu
subway	chikatetsu
suddenly	kyū-ni
sugar	satō
summer	natsu
sun	taiyō
Sunday	Nichiyōbi
sure	tashika (na)
(Are you) sure	Tashika desu-ka?
(to be) surprised	odoroku (odorokimasu)
sweater	suētā
sweet	amai
(to) swim	oyogu (oyogimasu)
sword	katana

T

table	tēburu
tailor	yōfukuya
Taiwan	Taiwan
Taiwanese	Taiwan-jin
(to) take	toru (torimasu)
(to) talk	hanasu (hanashimasu)
tall	takai
tank	tanku
tanker	tankā
tape	tēpu
tape recorder	tēpu rekōdā
(to) taste	ajiwau (ajiwaimasu)
tasty	oishii
taxi	takushīi
tea	o-cha
teahouse	chaya
(to) teach	oshieru (oshiemasu)
teacher	sensei
telegram	denpō
telephone	denwa
telivision	terebi
(to) tell	iu (iimasu)
Please tell him . . .	Kare ni itte kudasai . . .
Please tell her . . .	Kanojo ni itte kudasai . . .
temperature	ondo
temple	otera
ten	jū
tennis	tenisu
than	yori
Thank you!	Arigatō!
Many thanks!	Taihen arigatō!
that	(pro.) sore, (adj.) sono
their, theirs	karera-no

them	karera-o
(to) them	karera-ni
then	sore kara
there	asoko (or) asoko-ni
There is, There are	arimasu (for things)
Is there, Are there?	arimasu-ka (for things)
There isn't, There aren't	arimasen (for things)
There is, There are	imasu (for people, animals)
Is there, Are there?	imasu-ka (for people, animals)
There isn't, There aren't	imasen (for people, animals)
therefore	desu kara
these	korera (pronoun), korera-no (adjective)
thermometer	kandankei
they	karera
thick	futoi
thin	hosoi
thing	mono
(to) think	omou (omoimasu)
(to be) thirsty	nodo ga kawaita
thirteen	jūsan
thirty	sanjū
this (or) these	kono (adj.), kore (pro.)
those	sorerano (adj.), sorera (pro.)
thousand	sen
three	san (or) mittsu
through (over)	owari
Thursday	Mokuyōbi
ticket	kippu
tiger	tora
time	toki (or) jikan
What time is it?	Nan-ji desu-ka?
tip	chippu
tire	taiya
tired	tsukareta

to (direction)	e
to (indirect object)	-ni
today	kyō
toe	ashiyubi
together	to issho-ni
toilet	otearai
tomorrow	ashita (or) myōnichi
tongue	shita
tonight	konban
too (also)	mo
too (excessive)	amari
tool	dōgu
tooth	ha
toothbrush	ha burashi
total	gōkei
tour	kankō
tourist	kankō kyaku
towel	taoru
town	machi
toy	omocha
trade	shōgyō
traffic	kōtsū
train	kisha
transistor	toranjisutā
(to) translate	yakusu (yakushimasu)
Please translate!	Yakushite, kudasai!
(to) travel	ryokō suru (ryokō shimasu)
tree	ki
trip	ryokō
Have a good trip!	yoi ryokō-o dōzo!
trouble	kurō
trousers	zubon
truck	torakku
true	honto (no)
truly	honto (ni)

(to) try	yatte miru (yatte mimasu)
Tuesday	Kayōbi
tunnel	chikadō
(to) turn	mawaru (mawarimasu)
twelve	jūni
twenty	nijū
two	ni (or) futatsu
typewriter	taipuraitā
typical	dokutoku (na)
typhoon	taifū
typist	taipisuto

U

ugly	minikui
umbrella	kasa
uncle	oji
under	shita-ni
(to) understand	wakaru (wakarimasu)
Do you understand?	Wakarimasu-ka?
I don't understand.	Wakarimasen.
underwear	shitagi
unfortunately	ainiku
United Kingdom	Rengō Ōkoku
United Nations	Kokusai Rengō
United States of America	Amerika Gasshūkoku
university	daigaku
unlawful	fuhō (no)
unsafe	abunai
until	made
unusual	mezurashii
up	ue-ni

upstairs	ni kai (-ni)
urgent	kinkyū
us	watakushidomo-o
(to) us	watakushidomo-ni
(to) use	tsukau (tsukaimasu)
(to be) useful	yaku-ni tatsu (yaku-ni tachimasu)
useless	muyō (na)
usually	taigai

V

vacant	kara (no), kūkyo (na)
vacation	kyūka
valley	tani
valuable	daiji (na)
value	neuchi
various	shuju (no)
vegetable	yasai
very	taihen
view	keshiki
village	mura
vinegar	su
violin	baiorin
visa	biza (or) sashō
(to) visit	hōmon suru (hōmon shimasu)
voice	koe
volcano	kazan

W

(to) wait	matsu (machimasu)
Wait, please!	Matte, kudasai!
waiter	bōi-san
waitress	ojō-san
(to) walk	aruku (arukimasu)
wallet	saifu
(to) want	To express **"to want"** or **"to wish"** drop the *-masu* ending and add *-tai* followed by *desu*.
	I want to go. *Ikitai desu.*
	The negative is formed by changing *-tai desu* to *-taku nai*.
	I don't want to go. *Ikitaku nai.*
war	sensō
warehouse	sōko
warm	atatakai
was	deshita, imashita (or) arimashita
(to) wash	arau (araimasu)
watch	tokei
water	mizu
hot water	oyu
wave	nami
tidal wave	tsunami
way (manner)	hōhō
way (route)	hōkō, michi
one way	ippō-tsūkō
(to) wear	kiru (kimasu)
weather	tenki (or) tenkō
Wednesday	Suiyōbi
week	shūkan
last week	senshū
next week	raishū

this week	konshū
weight	mekata
gross weight	sōmekata
net weight	shōmimekata
Welcome! (on arriving)	Yoku irasshaimashita!
You are welcome!	Dō itashimashite!
well (water, oil)	ido
were	deshita, imashita (or) arimashita
west	nishi
whale	kujira
what	nani
What's the matter?	Dō shimashita-ka?
What is it?	Nan desu-ka?
What do you want?	Nani-ga hoshii desu-ka?
What is this in Japanese?	Kore-wa nihongo-de nan-to iimasu-ka?
wheel	kuruma (or) sharin
When?	Itsu desu-ka?
Where?	Doko?
where	doko
Where is . . . ?	. . . doko desu-ka?
Where to?	Doko-e?
which	dochira-no
while	aida
white	shiroi
who	dare
Who is it?	Dare desu-ka?
whom	dare-o
(To) whom?	dare-ni
whose	dare-no
Why?	Naze desu-ka?
wide	hiroi
(my) wife	kanai (or) tsuma
(your) wife	okusan
wind	kaze

window	mado
wine	budōshu
winter	fuyu
(to) wish	(see **to want**)
with	to (or) to issho-ni
without	nashi-ni
woman	onna
wonderful	subarashii
wood	ki
woods	hayashi
wool	keito
word	kotoba
work	shigoto
(to) work	hataraku (hatarakimasu)
world	sekai
(to) worry	shinpai suru (shinpai shimasu)
Don't worry!	Shinpai shinai!
worse	motto warui
wrist	tekubi
wristwatch	ude dokei
(to) write	kaku (kakimasu)
Please write it.	Sore-o kaite kudasai.
wrong	machigai

Y

year	nen (or) toshi
last year	sakunen
next year	rainen
this year	kommen (or) kotoshi
yellow	ki iro
yes	hai

yesterday	sakujitsu (or) kinō
not yet	mada
you	anata
you (direct object)	anata-o
(to) you, (for) you	anata-ni
young	wakai
your (or) **yours**	anata-no

Z

zero	rei
zigzag	giza giza
zone	kuiki
zoo	dōbutsuen

23. Point to the Answer

If you have asked a question in Japanese and do not understand the answer, show the Japanese person the paragraph immediately below, so he or she will know that you wish them to point to the answer to your question.

私 が 話している 相手 の 方 に：
理解 された 事 を 確かめる
為 に 私 の 質問 の 答 を こいで
見せて下さい. どうも 有難う.

は い	い い え	多 分
Hai	**Iie**	**Ta bun**
Yes	No	Perhaps

勿 論	大 丈 夫	すみません
Mochiron	**Dai jyō bu**	**Sumimasen**
Certainly	All right	Excuse me

解ります

Wakarimasu
I understand

解りません

Wakarimasen
I don't understand

何が欲しいですか?

Nani-ga hoshii desu-ka?
What do you want?

知ってます

Shitte imasu
I know

知りません

Shirimasen
I don't know

もう一度(又はもっと)

Mō ichi do
Again

Motto
More

充分です

Jyūbun desu
Enough

開ける

Akeru
Open

閉める

Shimeru
Closed

多すぎる

Ōsugiru
Too much

充分でない

Jyūbun de nai
Not enough

入場謝絶

Nyū jyō sha zetsu
No admittance

禁止の

Kin shi-no
It is forbidden

私有地

Shi yū chi
Private property

退去しなければなりません

Tai kyo shinakereba narimasen
You must leave

今

Ima
Now

後で

Ato de
Later

早過ぎる

Haya sugiru
Too early

遅すぎる

Oso sugiru
Too late

今日

Kyō
Today

明日

Ashita
Tomorrow

昨日

Kinō
Yesterday

今晩

Kon ban
Tonight

昨晩

Saku ban
Last night

明晩

Myō ban
Tomorrow night

今週

Kon shū
This week

先週

Sen shū
Last week

来週

Rai shū
Next week

可能です

Kanō desu
It's possible

不可能です

Fukanō desu
It's not possible

賛成した

Sansei shita
It is agreed

大変良い

Tai hen yoi
Very good

良くない

Yoku nai
It isn't good

近い

Chi kai
It's near

遠すぎる

Tō sugiru
Too far

大変遠い　此処

Taihen tōi
Very far

Koko
Here

あそこ

Asoko
There

左に曲る

Hidari-ni magaru
Turn left

右に曲る

Migi-ni magaru
Turn right

眞直ぐ行く

Massugu iku
Go straight ahead

私と一緒に来て

Watakushi-to issho-ni kite
Come with me

私の後について来る

Watakushi-no ato-ni tsuite kuru
Follow me

行きましょう

Ikima shō
Let's go

着きました

Tsukimashita
We have arrived

此処で止まる

Koko-de tomaru
Stop here

私を待って

Watakushi-o matte
Wait for me

出来ません

Dekimasen
I cannot

待ちます

Machimasu
I will wait

行かねばなりません

Ikane ba narimasen
I must go

後で戻ります

Ato-de modori masu
Come back later.

すぐ戻ります

Sugu modori masu
I'll be right back

彼は此処に居ません

Kare-wa koko-ni imasen
He is not here

彼女は此処に居ません

Kanojo-wa koko-ni imasen
She is not here.

私の名前は…..

Watakushi-no namae wa. . .
My name is. . .

貴方の名前は？

Anata-no namae wa?
Your name?

電話番号は？

Denwa bangō wa?
Telephone number?

住所は？

Jyū sho wa?
Address?

月曜（日）

Getsu yō (bi)
Monday

火曜（日）

Ka yō (bi)
Tuesday

水曜（日）

Sui yō (bi)
Wednesday

木曜（日）

Moku yō (bi)
Thursday

金曜（日）

Kin yō (bi)
Friday

土曜（日）

Do yō (bi)
Saturday

日曜（日）

Nichi yō (bi)
Sunday

…. 時に

. . . ji ni
At . . . o'clock

その値段は …..円 …. 銭です

Sono nedan wa . . . yen . . . sen desu
It costs . . . yen . . . sen

一
ichi
one

二
ni
two

三
san
three

四
shi
four

五
go
five

六
roku
six

七
shichi
seven

八
hachi
eight

九
ku
nine

十
jyū
ten

十一
jyū ichi
eleven

十二
jyū ni
twelve

十三
jyū san
thirteen

十四
jyū shi
fourteen

十五
jyū go
fifteen

十六
jyū roku
sixteen

十七
jyū shichi
seventeen

十八
jyū hachi
eighteen

十九
jyū ku
nineteen

二十
ni jyū
twenty

三十
san jyū
thirty

四十
shi jyū
forty

五十
go jyū
fifty

六十
roku jyū
sixty

七十
shichi jyū
seventy

八十
hachi jyū
eighty

九十
kyū jyū
ninety

百
hya ku
one hundred

千
sen
one thousand

万
man
ten thousand

Note: The Japanese used above is the way it is usually written, a combination of Sino-Japanese characters and the Hiragana script. The Hiragana uses the same syllable system as the Katakana (described on page 123), but most of the "letters" are written differently, and in a more cursive and graceful style.